# Living Green

**Recent Titles in
Q&A Health Guides**

Self-Injury: Your Questions Answered
*Romeo Vitelli*

Sexually Transmitted Diseases: Your Questions Answered
*Paul Quinn*

Anxiety and Panic Attacks: Your Questions Answered
*Daniel Zwillenberg*

# LIVING GREEN

## Your Questions Answered

Amy Hackney Blackwell

Q&A Health Guides

GREENWOOD™

An Imprint of ABC-CLIO, LLC

Santa Barbara, California • Denver, Colorado

Copyright © 2018 by ABC-CLIO, LLC

Library of Congress Cataloging in Publication Control Number: 2017046436

ISBN: 978-1-4408-5982-3 (print)
    978-1-4408-5983-0 (ebook)

22  21  20  19  18    1  2  3  4  5

This book is also available as an eBook.

Greenwood
An Imprint of ABC-CLIO, LLC

ABC-CLIO, LLC
130 Cremona Drive, P.O. Box 1911
Santa Barbara, California 93116–1911
www.abc-clio.com

This book is printed on acid-free paper ∞

Manufactured in the United States of America

# Contents

# Series Foreword

All of us have questions about our health. Is this normal? Should I be doing something differently? Who should I talk to about my concerns? And our modern world is full of answers. Thanks to the Internet, there's a wealth of information at our fingertips, from forums where people can share their personal experiences to Wikipedia articles to the full text of medical studies. But finding the right information can be an intimidating and difficult task—some sources are written at too high a level, others have been oversimplified, while still others are heavily biased or simply inaccurate.

*Q&A Health Guides* address the needs of readers who want accurate, concise answers to their health questions, authored by reputable and objective experts, and written in clear and easy-to-understand language. This series focuses on the topics that matter most to young adult readers, including various aspects of physical and emotional well-being, as well as other components of a healthy lifestyle. These guides will also serve as a valuable tool for parents, school counselors, and others who may need to answer teens' health questions.

All books in the series follow the same format to make finding information quick and easy. Each volume begins with an essay on health literacy and why it is so important when it comes to gathering and evaluating health information. Next, the top five myths and misconceptions that surround the topic are dispelled. The heart of each guide is a collection of questions and answers, organized thematically. A selection of five case studies provides real-world examples to illuminate key concepts. Rounding out each volume are a glossary, directory of resources, and index.

It is our hope that the books in this series will not only provide valuable information but also help guide readers toward a lifetime of healthy decision making.

# Introduction

At this point, everyone knows that climate change is a concern. Global temperatures are rising. Global carbon dioxide levels are rising. Global sea levels are rising. Scientists debate the details, but the consensus is real: the climate is changing and it is changing because of human actions.

The question is, what to do about it? How can one individual live sustainably and conserve and preserve the world's natural resources? Governments and businesses, motivated by varying combinations of public and financial interest, argue about this issue. Climate change, in particular, has been made a political football. It can be hard to discuss it in a rational manner because people are so emotionally invested in the issue. But the impact of human activities on the environment is actually measurable, and there are facts to apply to the matter.

Green living may appear to be a matter of lifestyle and politics, but the state of the environment is also one of the biggest health issues facing humans today. Increasing global temperatures have real effects on human health. People are literally dying at this very moment from air pollution in their cities. If you are concerned about health, you should think about how you live.

The objective of this book is to help clarify some of the key issues and give readers some ways to think about how they live. It does not begin to cover the full range of information or issues; people can do entire degrees in environmental science and policy. It is intended merely as a quick resource and a jumping-off point. Readers can and should investigate these issues more fully—the Internet abounds in good sources and active debate.

# Guide to Health Literacy

On her 13th birthday, Samantha was diagnosed with type 2 diabetes. She consulted her mom and her aunt, who both also have type 2 diabetes, and decided to go with their strategy of managing sugar by taking insulin. As a result of participating in an after-school program at her middle school that focused on health literacy, she learned that she can help manage the level of sugar in her bloodstream by counting her carbohydrate intake, following a diabetic diet, and exercising regularly. But what exactly should she do? How does she keep track of her carbohydrate intake? What is a diabetic diet? How long should she exercise and what type of exercise should she do? Samantha is a visual learner, so she turned to her favorite source of media, YouTube, to answer these questions. She found videos from individuals around the world sharing their experiences and tips, doctors (or at least people who have "Dr." in their YouTube channel names), government agencies such as the National Institutes of Health, and even video clips from cat lovers who have cats with diabetes. With guidance from the librarian and the health and science teachers at her school, she assessed the credibility of the information in these videos and even compared their suggestions to some of the print resources that she was able to find at her school library. Now, she knows exactly how to count her carbohydrate level, how to prepare and follow a diabetic diet, and how much (and what) exercise is needed daily. She intends to share her findings with her mom and her aunt and now wants to create a chart that summarizes what she has learned that she can share with her doctor.

Samantha's experience is not unique. She represents a shift in our society; an individual no longer views himself or herself as a passive recipient of medical care but as an active mediator of his or her own health. However, in this era where any individual can post his or her opinions and experiences with a particular health condition online with just a few clicks or publish a memoir, it is vital that people know how to assess the credibility of health information. Gone are the days when "publishing" health information required intense vetting. The health information landscape is highly saturated, and people have innumerable sources where they can find information about practically any health topic. The sources (whether print, online, or a person) that an individual consults for health information are crucial because the accuracy and trustworthiness of the information can potentially affect his or her overall health. The ability to find, select, assess, and use health information constitutes a type of literacy—health literacy—that everyone must possess.

## THE DEFINITION AND PHASES OF HEALTH LITERACY

One of the most popular definitions for health literacy comes from Ratzan and Parker (2000), who describe health literacy as "the degree to which individuals have the capacity to obtain, process, and understand basic health information and services needed to make appropriate health decisions." Recent research has extrapolated health literacy into health literacy bits, further shedding light on the multiple phases and literacy practices that are embedded within the multifaceted concept of health literacy. Although this research has focused primarily on online health information seeking, these health literacy bits are needed to successfully navigate both print and online sources. There are six phases of health information seeking: (1) information need identification and question formulation, (2) information search, (3) information comprehension, (4) information assessment, (5) information management, and (6) information use.

The first phase is *information need identification and question formulation*. In this phase, one needs to be able to develop and refine a range of questions to frame one's search and understand relevant health terms. In the second phase, *information search*, one has to possess appropriate searching skills, such as using proper keywords and correct spelling in search terms, especially when using search engines and databases. It is also crucial to understand how search engines work (i.e., how search results are derived, what the order of the search results means, how to use the snippets that are provided in the search results list to select websites, how to determine which listings are ads on a search engine results page). One also has to limit reliance on surface characteristics, such as the design of a website or a book (a website or book that appears to have a lot of information or looks aesthetically pleasant does not necessarily mean it has good information) and language used (a website or book that utilizes jargon, the keywords that one used to conduct the search, or the word "information" does not necessarily indicate it will have good information). The next phase is *information comprehension* whereby one needs to have the ability to read, comprehend, and recall the information (including textual, numerical, and visual content) one has located from the books and/or online resources.

To assess the credibility of health information (*information assessment* phase), one needs to be able to evaluate information for accuracy, evaluate how current the information is (e.g., when a website was last updated or when a book was published), and evaluate the creators of the source—for example, examine site sponsors or type of sites (.com, .gov, .edu, or .org) or the author of a book (practicing doctor, a celebrity doctor, a patient of a specific disease, etc.) to determine the believability of the person/organization providing the information. Such credibility perceptions tend to become generalized, so they must be frequently reexamined (e.g., the belief that a specific news agency always has credible health information needs continuous vetting). One also needs to evaluate the credibility of the medium (e.g., television, Internet, radio, social media, book) and evaluate—not just accept without questioning—others' claims regarding the validity of a site, book, or other specific source of information. At this stage, one has to "make sense of information gathered from diverse sources by identifying misconceptions, main and supporting ideas, conflicting information, point of view, and biases" (AASL, 2009, p. 13) and conclude which sources/information are valid and accurate by using conscious strategies rather than simply using intuitive judgments or "rules of thumb." This phase is the most challenging segment of health information seeking and serves as a determinant of success (or lack thereof) in the information-seeking process. The following section *Sources of Health Information* further explains this phase.

The fifth phase is *information management* whereby one has to organize information that has been gathered in some manner to ensure easy retrieval and use in the future. The last phase is *information use*, in which one will synthesize information found across various resources, draw conclusions, and locate the answer to his or her original question and/or the content that fulfills the information need. This phase also often involves implementation, such as using the information to solve a health problem, make health-related decisions, identify and engage in behaviors that will help a person to avoid health risks, share the health information found with family members and friends who may benefit from it, and advocate more broadly for personal, family, or community health.

## THE IMPORTANCE OF HEALTH LITERACY

The conception of health has moved from a passive view (someone is either well or ill) to one that is more active and process based (someone is working toward preventing or managing disease). Hence, the dominant focus has shifted from doctors and treatments to patients and prevention, resulting in the need to strengthen our ability and confidence (as patients and consumers of health care) to look for, assess, understand, manage, share, adapt, and use health-related information. An individual's health literacy level has been found to predict his or her health status better than age, race, educational attainment, employment status, and income level (National Network of Libraries of Medicine, 2013). Greater health literacy also enables individuals to better communicate with health-care providers such as doctors, nutritionists, and therapists, as they can pose more relevant, informed, and useful questions to health-care providers. Another added advantage of greater health literacy is better information-seeking skills, not only for health but also in other domains, such as completing assignments for school.

## SOURCES OF HEALTH INFORMATION: WHAT'S GOOD AND WHAT'S BAD AND THE IN-BETWEEN

For generations, doctors, nurses, nutritionists, health coaches, and other health professionals have been the trusted sources of health information. In addition, researchers have found that young adults, when they have health-related questions, typically turn to a family member who has had firsthand experience with a health condition because of their family member's close proximity and because of their past experience with, and trust in, this individual. Expertise should be a core consideration when consulting a person, website, or book for health information. The credentials and background of the person or author and conflicting interests of the author (and their organization) must be checked and validated to ensure the likely credibility of the health information they're conveying.

While books often have implied credibility because of the peer-review process involved, self-publishing has challenged this credibility, so qualifications of book authors should also be verified. When it comes to health information, currency of the source must also be examined. When examining health information/studies presented, pay attention to the exhaustiveness of research methods utilized to offer recommendations or conclusions. Small and nondiverse sample size is often—but not always—an indication of reduced credibility. Studies that confuse correlation with causation is another potential issue to watch for. Information seekers must also pay attention to the sponsors of the research studies. For example, if a study is sponsored by manufacturers of drug Y and the study recommends that drug Y is the best treatment to manage or cure a disease, this may indicate a lack of objectivity on the part of the researchers.

The Internet is rapidly becoming one of the main sources of health information. Online forums, news agencies, personal blogs, social media sites, pharmacy sites, and celebrity "doctors" are all offering medical and health information targeted at various types of people in regard to all types of diseases and symptoms. There are professional journalists, citizen journalists, hoaxers, and people paid to write fake health news on various sites that may appear to have a legitimate domain name and may even have authors who claim to have professional credentials, such as an MD. All these sites *may* offer useful information or information that appears to be useful and relevant; however, much of the information may be debatable and may fall into gray areas that require readers to discern credibility, reliability, and biases.

While broad recognition and acceptance of certain media, institutions, and people often serve as the most popular determining factors to assess credibility of health information among young people, keep in mind that there are legitimate Internet sites, databases, and books that publish health information and serve as sources of health information for doctors, other health sites, and members of the public. For example, MedlinePlus (https://medlineplus.gov) has trusted sources on over 975 diseases and conditions and presents the information in easy-to-understand language.

Some factors to consider when assessing credibility of health information are provided in the chart. However, keep in mind that these factors function only as a guide and require continuous updating to keep abreast with the changes in the landscape of health information, information sources, and technologies.

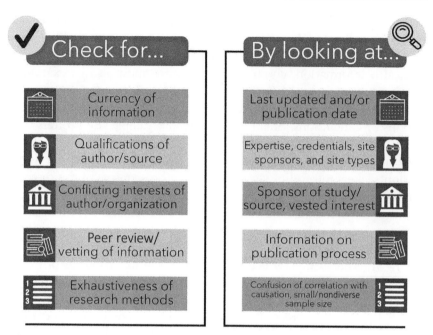

All images from flaticon.com

The chart can serve as a guide; however, approaching a librarian about how one can go about assessing the credibility of both print and online health information is far more effective than using generic checklist-type tools. While librarians are not health experts, they can apply and teach patrons strategies to determine the credibility of health information.

With the prevalence of fake sites and fake resources that appear to be legitimate, it is important to use the following health information assessment tips to verify health information that one has obtained (St. Jean et al., 2015, p. 151):

- *Don't assume you're right*: Even when you feel very sure about an answer, keep in mind that the answer may not be correct and it is important to conduct (further) searches to validate the information.
- *Don't assume you're wrong*: You may actually have correct information, even if the information you encounter does not match—that is, you may be right and the resources that you have found may contain false information.
- *Take an open approach*: Maintain a critical stance by not including your preexisting beliefs as keywords (or letting them influence your

choice of keywords) in a search, as this may influence what it is possible to find out.

- *Verify, verify, verify*: Information found, especially on the Internet, needs to be validated, no matter how the information appears on the site (i.e., regardless of the appearance of the site or the quantity of information that is included).

Health literacy comes with experience navigating health information. Professional sources of health information, such as doctors, health-care providers, and health databases, are still the best, but one also has the power to search for health information and then verify it by consulting with these trusted sources and by using the health information assessment tips and guide shared earlier.

Mega Subramaniam, PhD
Associate Professor, College of Information Studies,
University of Maryland

## REFERENCES AND FURTHER READING

American Association of School Librarians (AASL). (2009). *Standards for the 21st-century learner in action.* Chicago, IL: American Association of School Librarians.

Hilligoss, B., & Rieh, S.-Y. (2008). Developing a unifying framework of credibility assessment: Construct, heuristics, and interaction in context. *Information Processing & Management, 44*(4), 1467–1484.

Kuhlthau, C. C. (1988). Developing a model of the library search process: Cognitive and affective aspects. *Reference Quarterly, 28*(2), 232–242.

National Network of Libraries of Medicine (NNLM). (2013). Health Literacy. National Network of Libraries of Medicine, Bethesda, MD. Retrieved from nnlm.gov/outreach/consumer/hlthlit.html

Ratzan, S. C., & Parker, R. M. (2000). Introduction. In C. R. Selden, M. Zorn, S. C. Ratzan, & R. M. Parker (Eds.), *National Library of Medicine Current Bibliographies in Medicine: Health Literacy.* NLM Pub. No. CBM 2000-1. Bethesda, MD: National Institutes of Health, U.S. Department of Health and Human Services.

St. Jean, B., Subramaniam, M., Taylor, N. G., Follman, R., Kodama, C., & Casciotti, D. (2015). The influence of positive hypothesis testing on youths' online health-related information seeking. *New Library World, 116*(3/4), 136–154.

St. Jean, B., Taylor, N. G., Kodama, C., & Subramaniam, M. (in press). Assessing the health information source perceptions of tweens using card-sorting exercises. *Journal of Information Science.*

Subramaniam, M., St. Jean, B., Taylor, N. G., Kodama, C., Follman, R., and Casciotti, D. (2015). Bit by bit: Using design-based research to improve the health literacy of adolescents. *JMIR Research Protocols,* 4(2), paper e62. Retrieved from http://www.ncbi.nlm.nih.gov/pmc/articles/PMC4464334/

Valenza, J. (2016, November 26). Truth, truthiness, and triangulation: A news literacy toolkit for a "post-truth" world [web log]. Retrieved from http://blogs.slj.com/neverendingsearch/2016/11/26/truth-truthiness-triangulation-and-the-librarian-way-a-news-literacy-toolkit-for-a-post-truth-world/

# Common Misconceptions
## about Living Green

## 1. THERE'S NOTHING I CAN DO TO MAKE A DIFFERENCE

Everything you do makes a difference. That's basic ecology. The carbon dioxide you exhale, the nitrogen you excrete in urine, the animals you eat—all of that goes into the ecological mix. Ecological systems run on inputs of energy and materials and outputs of wastes. Human society is no exception. The problem is that there are so many people on the planet, so many businesses producing goods and polluting the air, that it seems that nothing you can do will make a real dent in the environmental problems they cause. So why should you bother to live green? You don't have to. But it's nice to live consciously. You can choose how you want to live, and living green is a valid option. For more information, see Questions 1 and 13 for a start.

## 2. RENEWABLE ENERGY CAN'T MEET ENOUGH ENERGY NEEDS TO BE PRACTICAL

In fact, renewables are already providing the majority of power in numerous countries. Naysayers insist that nothing provides power like fossil fuels. This is partly due to the entrenched advantages of fossil fuel providers, who have dominated the market for decades. As of 2017, developed nations (the G20 nations) provided four times more public financing to fossil fuels than to renewable energy. But times are changing. There are very good reasons for countries to decrease dependence on coal and oil: air pollution, climate change, oil spills, threat of foreign war, money. Energy technology is developing rapidly. Smart integration of different sources of renewable energy can prevent gaps in power. Greenpeace has declared the world ready for a clean energy revolution; by all indications, we are already in the midst of it. For more on renewables, see Questions 9, 12, 13, and the other topics in the Power section.

## 3. GREEN LIVING IS TOO EXPENSIVE

The fact is green living can cost much less than nongreen living. At its most basic, green living means owning only what you actually need. Own five pairs of shoes instead of 20, and replace them only when you need to. Instead of buying clothing at a retail store, you might get used garments from a consignment shop. If you don't tumble dry your clothes, you don't need to buy a drier or to pay for electricity to run the one you own. Eco-friendly transportation—walking, biking, taking the bus or train, ride-sharing—almost always costs less than buying your own car and filling it with gasoline. You have choices. If you take the trouble to learn about the real costs and benefits of those choices, then you can decide how to live based on real information. For more on practical life choices, see Questions 23–25, 31, 36, and 38.

## 4. THE CLIMATE CHANGES ALL THE TIME NATURALLY: HUMAN ACTIVITIES DON'T AFFECT IT MUCH

Climate does change all the time. It changes for specific reasons. Those reasons in the past have included plants performing photosynthesis, massive volcanic eruptions, and accidents involving asteroids. There is no reason humans burning fossil fuels can't change the climate too. Today we humans are pulling 300 million years' worth of carbon out of the earth and putting it back in the air. This, of course, makes a difference to how much heat the atmosphere can hold. Remember, if plants alone could bring on a planetary ice age, humans are more than capable of changing the climate. For more information on climate change, see Questions 3–5.

## 5. TECHNOLOGY WILL SAVE HUMANITY FROM ENVIRONMENTAL PROBLEMS

Thomas Malthus (1766–1834), an English demographer, wrote that increasing food led to increased population, which would eventually outstrip available resources. The end result would be mass deaths in a catastrophe such as famine or disease. Looking at human population growth—1.6 billion in 1900, 6 billion in 1999, 7 billion by 2011 (or 2012), with another billion forecast by 2025—it's hard not to wonder if we are in fact heading for a crisis. And yet humans today live better than they ever have. Won't our ingenuity save us as the environment changes? The question, though, is whether technology can keep pace. Our power grids and transportation structures are very vulnerable to disruption from natural disasters. Technology has produced some amazing things. But it is also worth remembering just how vulnerable we are. For more on the dangers of environmental problems, see Questions 7 and 11, among others.

# QUESTIONS AND ANSWERS

---

❖

# Basics

### 1. What is "green living"?

So you want to live green. What exactly does that mean?
Here are a few definitions:

> Green living is a lifestyle that tries in as many ways as it can to bring into balance the conservation and preservation of the Earth's natural resources, habitats, and biodiversity *with* human culture and communities. . . . In laymen's terms, living green and sustainably means creating a lifestyle that works with Nature, instead of against it, and does no long-term or irreversible damage to any part of the environmental web. (Sustainable Baby Steps website)

> Green living means:

> Understanding that the choices you make affect not just you, but everybody everywhere. Understanding that the choices you make affect not just today, but the future. Understanding that when we talk about "saving the planet" or "saving the environment," we are actually talking about saving ourselves! (PBSKids)

> Green living is a state of mind. If you are living green you are probably concerned about the environment, eating healthy, fair trade labor practices, buying local, and activism. People who are living

green generally do a lot of research about topics which affect their health and/or health of others. If you are living green you are most likely making conscious choices about all aspects of your life and are eager to learn and share your experiences. (Urban Dictionary)

Often "green living" is intertwined with "sustainability." Green living websites suggest that we "reduce, reuse, recycle"; they recommend eating organic, locally grown food; they fret about water and air pollution. A person who lives green might drive less, use renewable energy, read food labels, shop with his or her own cloth bags, conserve water, and live in a green home.

Many nations have some version of a Green Party, a political party that makes environmental protection a top priority. Greens also tend to favor social justice, human rights, gender and racial equality, animal welfare, and consumer protection. Greens tend to be progressive, anticapitalist, and antiwar. The U.S. Green Party is quite small compared to the Democratic and Republican parties that dominate U.S. pólitics, and it has not had much electoral success (partly due to laws that favor established political parties in elections), but it has gotten a certain amount of press. It is most popular in the Northeast and Wisconsin and on the Pacific Coast.

Of course, you can't always trust the word "green," which has been incorporated into a range of uses. Look out for the nefarious greenwashing—the use of the word "green" to sell products to environmentally minded consumers, whether or not those products are actually green.

Green living owes a great deal to the discipline of ecology, the study of the interactions of organisms with their living and nonliving environments. The name "ecology" comes from the Greek words *oikos*, or "home," and *logia*, or "study"—so ecology is the study of our home. The most fundamental principle of ecology is that no organism exists independently of other living and nonliving things around it.

Every organism is part of an ecosystem. It draws energy and resources from its environment and changes its environment by its own existence and death. Energy for life initially comes from the sun, and then through plants, which can use light energy to make their own food. That energy then flows through the animals that eat plants and animals that eat animals.

The ultimate goal of ecology is to understand the nature of environmental influences on individual organisms, their populations, and communities; on landscapes; and, ultimately, on all life on Earth. By this standard, living green means paying attention—paying attention to where things come from, where they go, and what that process costs.

For example, if you order a hamburger at McDonald's, you might consider how many resources go into getting that hamburger to you—water and feed for cattle, farms and fertilizer for grain, slaughterhouses and processing plants, fuel to propel trucks down the highway, electricity to run the air conditioning, wood cut down to make a paper bag that you toss in the trash so it can go to a landfill where it will simply sit and never decompose. That thought process can then help you make decisions about what to do. You may still choose to eat the hamburger—maybe it's the only food available, you are traveling with small children and need a playground, or you really love McDonald's hamburgers—but you will make that choice aware of what it costs.

The aluminum can that contains a soft drink did not materialize for free just for your momentary drinking pleasure. It came from somewhere—someone spent money and effort to make it—and it goes somewhere after you are done with it. Maybe you don't think the use of aluminum to temporarily hold sugary drinks is a problem. Maybe you do.

Why care about preserving endangered species, even the ones that have no use to humans? Aside from the fact that a human use might appear in the future, all organisms are part of ecosystems and contribute to the way they function. The loss of one species can drastically change the way an entire ecosystem works.

Why care about carbon emissions? That one is easy—they are making the planet hotter, and that is already causing problems for humans. If you take the trouble to study the issue, you can decide for yourself how best to respond.

Different people take different viewpoints on green issues. Many believe wholeheartedly in the importance of being environmentally aware and making green decisions. Others believe just the opposite, arguing that attempting to protect the environment costs too much and isn't necessary anyway. If you want to live green, you will find plenty of arguments against your positions—but you will also find plenty of well-informed company.

People who consider themselves environmentalists often have a hard time reconciling their various actions. What if you refuse to eat meat but still wear leather shoes—does that make you a bad vegan? If you don't drive a car but fly every week, how are you helping the environment? Why bother recycling if you visit Starbucks every day for coffee with a disposable cup and lid? How can you manage to be an environmentalist if you live someplace with no public transportation at all? Does it make sense to spend money on ethically produced clothing when Walmart sells the clothing for one-fifth the price?

And individuals do matter. Rachel Carson launched an entire environmental movement with her 1962 book *Silent Spring*. Thanks to her, the pesticide DDT is no longer prevalent in the environment, causing birds of prey to lay eggs with impossibly thin shells. Environmental activists have changed laws and fashions. Citizen protests can get governments and corporations to change their ways.

Although the notion of green living may once have given off a hippie vibe, these days you do not have to eat granola and wear Birkenstocks to be interested in green living. There are definite economic reasons to live green—conserving resources and polluting less—that do not require you to adopt certain political views. Plenty of economically powerful people on all parts of the political spectrum see the value in protecting the environment. Living green is possible for anyone.

## 2. What is "sustainability"?

Sustainability is the use of resources and development of practices in a way that meets the needs of people alive today without making it impossible for future generations to meet those same needs.

Our very survival could be at stake. Throughout human history, societies have collapsed when they were unable to produce enough food. For example, the Dust Bowl of the 1930s was caused by poor farming practices combined with a drought. Most of the soil in Oklahoma dried up and blew away. No one could farm anymore, and thousands of people nearly starved to death. The Dust Bowl was the result of unsustainable practices interacting with natural phenomena.

The U.S Environmental Protection Agency (EPA) points out that everything humans need to survive depends on the natural environment. If humans are to thrive in the future, we need to be careful about how we use natural resources today.

Sustainability does not mean giving up all human activities. Instead, it means finding ways to allow for economic development without damaging the environment so much that human life becomes difficult or impossible. Sustainability needs to include economic and social development along with environmental protection.

In 2015 the United Nations adopted 17 goals for sustainable development. These include an end to hunger and poverty, good health for all, clean water, affordable and clean energy, protection of the environment, and action to combat climate change. Climate change is a particular problem, because it causes rising sea levels that will eventually swamp coastal areas, including major cities, along with extreme weather events that will cause serious economic damage.

Sustainable urban development will be vital to a world in which increasing numbers of people live in cities. Transport systems such as trains and busses, energy production, and information technology will all be part of sustainable industrial development. Renewable energy is more sustainable than the use of fossil fuels because fossil fuels are irreplaceable; once coal or petroleum is burned, it is gone, but solar power is available whenever the sun shines.

Sustainability requires efficiency and an end of waste. About one-third of the food produced is wasted. Our current disposable culture wastes huge amounts of natural resources—think of all the money sunk into packaging that goes straight to a landfill. A sustainable food production system would produce enough food to feed the human population without excess waste. Sustainable development would maintain the fertility of the soil and the quality of the air and water.

A circular economy, in which durable goods are built to last longer and their materials are recycled, would make better use of resources. Business models in which people pay only for what they use—for example, paying someone to drive them instead of owning cars that mostly sit idle—would make consumption less wasteful.

Environmental protection is at the heart of sustainable development. This means preventing deforestation and desertification (the creation of deserts by degrading land). Humans still depend on natural life forms— plants and animals—for food. Many other plants and animals are essential to maintaining the health of forests and other wild areas. Fish and other marine animals are essential for human diets. All of these things are under threat. Hundreds of plant and animal species are endangered or extinct, and wild land disappears every day.

We depend on the natural world for the basics of existence. We cannot make our own water, and our food comes from natural processes done by plants and animals. Clean air is essential for human respiration, and humans can thrive only in a fairly small range of temperatures. Sustainability aims to preserve all the aspects of the environment that make human life possible.

## 3. What's the deal with carbon?

Carbon (C) is an element that makes up most of the bodies and tissues of living organisms. It is the 4th most abundant element in the universe, the 15th most abundant element on Earth, and the 2nd most abundant element in the human body. An atom of carbon has six protons. It has four valence electrons (electrons in its outermost shell), which makes it unusually able to form bonds with other atoms; carbon can form more compounds than any other element. Organic chemistry is the study of carbon; an organic molecule is a molecule that contains carbon.

The fossil fuels that currently supply 80 percent of our energy consist mainly of carbon, mixed with hydrogen—hence the name "hydrocarbon." Carbon is the main component of greenhouse gases, especially carbon dioxide and methane. When we burn fuels, their carbon enters the air as these gases, and the gases trap heat near Earth's surface. This is the main cause of the current increase in global temperatures.

To understand why this matters, you need to know a little about how plants work. Basically, plants make themselves out of air.

Plants generate their own "food" through a process called photosynthesis. When the sun shines on them, plants suck in carbon dioxide through pores in their leaves and then use light energy to convert that carbon dioxide into sugars, water, and oxygen. The oxygen and water leave the plant as waste products. The sugars, which are mostly carbon, turn into the plant's leaves, branches, flowers, fruits, and roots. Most of any plant is carbon.

When a plant takes in carbon dioxide, most of the carbon stays in the plant until it decays or something else happens to it. If it decays, some carbon goes back into the air and the rest turns into soil. If an animal eats a plant, the plant's carbon becomes the animal's carbon—it can become flesh or be excreted as waste. If, instead, the plant gets buried and compressed, that carbon stays underground.

Carbon cycles continuously from one form to another, from the air to plants to animals to soil and back to the air. A sink is a form of carbon that stores the element as a solid or liquid. Forests and oceans are sinks, which take carbon out of the air and hold it. A source gives off carbon as gases such as carbon dioxide and methane. Anything that burns carbon-based fuels and emits carbon dioxide into the atmosphere is a source; this includes automobiles, coal-fueled electrical power plants, and wood fires.

The plants and other organisms that supplied the carbon that makes up our current supply of fossil fuels died between 360 and 300 hundred million years ago. The carbon they pulled out of the air when they were alive has been buried since then, hidden deep underground. It has not been participating in the carbon cycle. Our fossil fuel reserves are a massive carbon sink.

Carbon dioxide levels have gone up and down throughout Earth's history. The reason people are now paying attention to carbon is that we humans have disrupted the carbon cycle and rapidly changed the atmosphere. For the past two centuries, people have been taking that long-stored carbon out of the ground and burning it for fuel. Since the 1860s, the use of coal, petroleum, and natural gas has released almost 300 billion tons of carbon into the air.

This additional carbon is making a real difference. Scientists at the Mauna Loa Observatory in Hawaii track levels of carbon in the air. Their measurements show a steady climb since 1956. In early 2017, carbon levels were up to 407 ppm (parts per million), a level not seen on Earth for millions of years and far too much for our current sinks to absorb. Methane, too, has been increasing. Carbon dioxide is responsible for more than 60 percent of the greenhouse effect, and methane accounts for another 20 percent.

Humans are adapted to living in a fairly narrow range of temperatures, as are many of the organisms inhabiting the planet with us. A sudden, large increase in temperatures is going to endanger many of the planet's current inhabitants.

Almost all human activities add carbon dioxide and methane to the atmosphere. Power plants spew out large amounts every year. Cars powered by gasoline emit tons of carbon dioxide. Airplanes are another culprit. Even simple wood fires add carbon to the air.

A carbon footprint is a measurement of the total greenhouse emissions caused by a business, person, activity, or anything else that emits carbon. Usually carbon footprint measures both carbon dioxide and methane. In the United States, the average household has a carbon footprint of about 50 tons per year—five times the worldwide average. The single biggest contributor to emissions is driving.

Some people think pulling carbon back out of the air and trapping it in sinks is a solution to the carbon problem. Planting forests to suck in carbon is one possible approach, though it is a slow process. Scientists have developed technologies that power plants can use to capture their emissions called carbon capture and sequestration. This process involves catching carbon emissions and injecting them deep underground instead of letting them get into the atmosphere. Though the technology is expensive, some states have begun implementing it in power plants.

National governments use carbon trading to regulate the total amount of carbon emitted. Each participating country that allows a certain amount of carbon emissions gets permits. Countries that do not emit their full allotment of carbon can sell their permits to countries that want to emit more. The idea behind emissions trading is that it sets an economic price on emissions, so that polluters can feel the full cost of their emissions and be encouraged to reduce them.

## 4. Is climate change real?

Yes. Anthropogenic climate change—climate change caused by human actions—is also real. There is no debate about this in the scientific community.

Climate change is a normal phenomenon. Earth's climate has changed many times over the planet's 4.54 billion years of existence. The composition of the atmosphere has not always been what it is now, about 21 percent oxygen and 78 percent nitrogen, with small amounts of other gases including carbon dioxide and methane. The composition of the atmosphere combined with the shape of landmasses, ocean currents, the size of ice sheets (which affects how much sunlight gets reflected or absorbed), volcanic eruptions, the occasional asteroid, and even changes in Earth's orbit affects global temperatures. Just 15,000 years ago much of the planet was covered with ice sheets and glaciers. Believe it or not, we are technically still in an ice age, just in a warm period called an interglacial.

The composition of the atmosphere is a very big factor in Earth's climate. Certain gases hold the sun's heat close to the surface; these gases are called greenhouse gases, because they hold in heat like the glass walls of a greenhouse. Carbon dioxide and methane are both greenhouse gases, so is water vapor. Greenhouse gases are a good thing—we need for the planet to be fairly warm and for temperatures to be consistent. Without greenhouse gases, our climate would be more like that on Mars, where temperatures are high when the sun is shining during the day but very low at night when it is not.

Earth's first atmosphere came from underground. Volcanoes erupted constantly, spewing carbon dioxide, methane, and hydrogen sulfide into the air. The first living organisms didn't need oxygen to live, which was good because there wasn't any oxygen in the air. Photosynthesis appeared about 3.5 billion years ago, when microorganisms called cyanobacteria developed the ability to make their own food from air using energy from the sun. Photosynthesis gives off oxygen as a waste product, so plants and cyanobacteria are the source of the oxygen we need to breathe.

Since then, the composition of the atmosphere has gone back and forth between high levels of oxygen and high levels of carbon dioxide. Land plants started spreading about 470 million years ago; after 30 million years or so, they had sucked enough carbon dioxide out of the air to trigger an ice age.

Fossil fuels are made of carbon that came from plants and algae that lived hundreds of millions of years ago. The last time the carbon in those fuels was in the air was before the dinosaurs even appeared. We've tossed it all back out over just two centuries. This is a massive rapid change to atmospheric composition. Increasing temperatures are closely tied to this release of long-hidden carbon.

The World Health Organization (WHO) calls climate change "the defining issue for the 21st century." It estimated in 2014 that the health impacts of climate change were causing about 150,000 deaths per year; by 2040, that number will have risen to 250,000. Those deaths will be due to heat stress, malnutrition (from failed crops), diarrhea (from unsanitary water), and malaria. Increased levels of pollen and ozone will increase respiratory ailments. Elderly people will be endangered by hot summers, such as the summer heat wave that killed 70,000 in Europe in 2003. Developing nations will be hit the hardest. Within the United States, climate change will affect the poorer states first and worst, with the poorest third (mostly the South and West, which are already hot) likely to sustain economic damage amounting to a fifth of their incomes. This damage is not likely to disappear, either.

## 5. Are global temperatures increasing or not?

Yes. Global temperatures are increasing.

The decade between 2002 and 2012 was the hottest ever recorded. June 2015 set a record for the highest average temperature over global land and sea surfaces. That record was broken by the temperatures in June 2016. June 2016 was the 34th June in a row in which temperatures were above average.

Earth's average surface temperature has steadily increased since about 1900. The National Aeronautics and Space Administration (NASA), the National Oceanic and Atmospheric Administration, and the Intergovernmental Panel on Climate Change, among many other scientific bodies, have created detailed pictures of climate history, and their conclusions are clear: global temperature is rising, and it is rising fast.

Global temperatures rose 350 million years ago, when early plants spread across the land and absorbed more sunlight than had been the case before. As those plants lowered carbon dioxide levels through photosynthesis, though, the greenhouse effect weakened and Earth's surface got colder.

During the Mesozoic Era (252–66 million years ago), dinosaurs inhabited a planet that was several degrees warmer than it is now, possibly because the configuration of landmasses at the time allowed global winds and ocean currents to distribute heat efficiently between the Equator and the poles. Our current era, the Cenozoic (which started 66 million years ago), has seen several climate ups and downs. When it began, Earth had no polar ice caps. During the Cenozoic the planet has gone through several ice ages, long periods when the planet is cold and parts of the surface are covered with ice.

We are actually in the midst of an ice age right now. It began about 2.6 million years ago. We happen to be in an interglacial, a period in which the ice sheets and glaciers retreat. The last glacial period, which is sometimes called an ice age, ended about 15,000 years ago. Human civilization as we know it was born and grew after the glaciers receded. Even since then, there have been small fluctuations in climate, with warm periods followed by cold spells.

So why does anyone worry about the increase in global temperatures today? Well, at the moment the increase is happening very quickly, and it is almost entirely attributable to human activity. Humans have been burning fossil fuels such as coal and petroleum for a very short time relative to the history of civilization—about 200 years of fossil fuel use compared to 12,000 or so years of agriculture—and already temperatures have increased noticeably. Just to compare, according to NASA, global temperatures increased 4–7°C in the 5,000 years after the last glaciers receded. In the past century, temperatures have increased 0.7°C—10 times the rate of that previous increase.

Climate models predict that temperatures will increase between 2°C and 6°C over the next 100 years—up to 20 times the post-glaciation rate of increase. The last time temperatures increased that much, it took thousands of years.

This rising temperature is going to be a problem. It has already caused noticeable changes to the weather. Spring 2017 came three weeks earlier than normal. The ice sheets on Antarctica and Greenland are melting rapidly. Glaciers are receding in the Alps and Himalayas. Rising temperatures will cause more extreme weather, along with heat waves, floods, droughts, and strong storms.

Even if we end all carbon emissions right now, global temperatures will keep rising, because the warming trend follows the addition of carbon to the atmosphere. And carbon emissions are not likely to end or even decrease much in the near-future. So expect the temperature to keep rising.

## 6. Why is the ozone layer important?

Ozone is a type of oxygen that contains three oxygen atoms per molecule, written with the chemical formula $O_3$. The oxygen we breathe consists of two oxygen atoms per molecule, written with the chemical formula $O_2$. Most of the oxygen in the atmosphere is diatomic oxygen, $O_2$, which is the stable form. Ozone is not very stable and is constantly trying to get rid of its extra oxygen atom to go back to being $O_2$.

Ozone constantly forms and breaks down in the atmosphere. It is produced when oxygen molecules react with solar radiation. Ultraviolet light from the sun strikes molecules of $O_2$ and splits them into individual oxygen atoms. These molecules do not like to be solitary, so they bind with molecules of $O_2$ to form $O_3$, ozone. The same ultraviolet light then breaks up the molecules of ozone, creating a never-ending cycle.

Most of this happens in the stratosphere, the part of the upper atmosphere between 9 and 18 miles above Earth's surface. In consequence, the stratosphere contains a concentrated layer of ozone.

Ozone is important because of the way it interacts with ultraviolet light. Ultraviolet (UV) radiation is a normal part of the spectrum of radiation that comes from the sun. It has smaller wavelengths than violet and blue light. It is invisible to the human eye, but human skin can feel it. Ultraviolet radiation causes sunburn. It can damage the DNA in the skin and cause cancer. It can also hurt plants and animals, which do not do well in conditions that resemble permanent tanning beds.

The ozone up in the stratosphere functions as a massive sun shield. All those chemical reactions that cycle oxygen through its various forms are powered by ultraviolet radiation, absorbed by atoms and molecules. The UV radiation that gets absorbed in the stratosphere does not make it to Earth's surface and thus cannot cause damage.

Without the ozone layer, too much UV radiation would reach the ground. This already happens in some places. Australia receives about 15 percent more UV radiation every year than Europe. This is partly because the Southern Hemisphere is closer to the sun during its summer than the Northern Hemisphere is, but it is also because the ozone layer there is thinner.

The ozone layer is thin over Australia because it is near the Antarctic, where there is actually a hole in the ozone. In 1984 scientists realized that every summer (Antarctic summer, i.e., December), a hole was forming in the ozone layer over the South Pole. They discovered that the ozone had been destroyed by chemicals called chlorofluorocarbons (CFCs), which were widely used in refrigeration and aerosols in the 1970s. When CFCs reach the stratosphere, they break down into chlorine molecules that bind with oxygen, disrupting the ozone cycle.

CFCs were banned by an international agreement called the Montreal Protocol, which took effect in 1989. The ozone layer is no longer deteriorating, but scientists expect that the Antarctic hole will not close until around 2070.

In the meantime, Australians suffer from the highest rates of skin cancer in the world. Doctors predict that two-thirds of Australians will receive a diagnosis of skin cancer during their lifetimes.

## 7. What does the government do to protect the environment?

To appreciate the value of government in environmental issues, consider the problem of poop. More specifically, think about poop in your drinking water.

Feces gets into the water supply when people defecate in the open. Water contaminated with feces is one of the leading causes of diarrhea, cholera, polio, typhoid, trachoma, schistosomiasis, and intestinal worms. According to the WHO, 842,000 people worldwide die every year from inadequate water, hygiene, and sanitation.

People left to their own devices aren't capable of building large systems and may see no reason to stop squatting behind bushes as they have always done. The slum dwellers of Lagos, Nigeria, are in no position to handle mass sanitation. This is where government comes in. Improved sanitation facilities, such as flush toilets and sewer systems or at least dug latrines, are almost always the work of governments.

A pioneer family in the woods might be able to get away without government because everything they need is available—they can hunt wild animals, gather wild plants, dip water from a wild stream. Maybe they grow a vegetable garden or raise chickens and pigs, which they butcher themselves.

Once people move to a town or city, though, they have to share. Farming, hunting, and getting water are all more complicated when many people want to use the same resources. We have government to manage the sharing.

Say, for example, a town has an open field. Townspeople let their cows graze on this field. No one pays for this service. The field can support 10 cows without suffering loss of grass. Any more than that leads to overgrazing and deterioration of the land.

If there are 10 townspeople and each one has one cow, then the situation is stable. But what if one person suddenly gets two more cows? The grass on the field is free and no one tells him or her not to, so that person lets his or her three cows loose to eat. With 13 cattle, the field is soon overgrazed and becomes useless. The group as a whole suffers because one person took more than his or her share of a joint resource.

This is called the tragedy of the commons. It is an economic theory that describes situations in which a shared resource can be destroyed by individuals acting in their own self-interest at the cost of the interests of the group. It can be applied to any situation in which a shared resource is unregulated. Fisheries, for example, can be rapidly depleted if each fishing boat takes as many fish as it can. A river can be drained dry if each farm along its course takes as much water as it wants.

People invented government to deal with this problem.

Laws and regulations can guide the use of resources that everyone uses so that no single individual or business can exploit them to the detriment of the population as a whole. Environmental regulation is very much guided by the desire to avoid the tragedy of the commons. It is especially important when large businesses profit from unregulated resources.

For example, the United States has had problems with air pollution since the late 1800s. By the first half of the 20th century, soot from burning coal blighted the air in many cities. As electricity and motor vehicles became more common, air pollution and smog became serious problems. The U.S. Congress passed the Clean Air Act in 1970 and has amended it several times since then. This law regulates air pollutants emitted by industry, motor vehicles, and other sources. The Clean Air Act has resulted in measurably better air since it was passed; air quality in the 2010s was better than that in 1980 despite decades of development.

Between the late 1960s and the 1990s, Congress passed several laws limiting the discharge of pollutants. Laws regulating emissions and pollutants are always politically challenging, and large polluters tend to resist any efforts to make them contain their emissions. In addition to the Clean Air Acts, laws regulating pollutants include the Safe Drinking Water Act, the Clean Water Act, and the Toxic Substances Control Act.

The United States Environmental Protection Agency (EPA) is the U.S. government's agency in charge of protecting the environment and human health. Its mission is to protect Americans from risks to their health that could be caused by environmental problems and to make human communities and ecosystems both economically and ecologically sustainable. The EPA helps write and enforce environmental laws, assesses environmental issues, sets national standards, and works with industry to reduce pollution and create sustainable practices.

The EPA is especially important when it comes to regulating industry. Businesses have an incentive to maximize profits that sometimes come at the expense of the environment. Government agencies are often the organizations best able to hold businesses accountable. For example, in 2015 it was discovered that Volkswagen and several other car manufacturers systematically cheated on their emissions tests for years, fooling thousands of customers into believing that they were driving pollution-free cars when in fact their cars were spewing deadly nitrogen oxide emissions. People are dying today because of this dishonesty. The EPA regularly tests car emissions to verify that they meet legal standards and has the power to issue notices of violation to manufacturers. Individuals can't do that.

Environmental protection is really a global issue, and the world's nations have been working for decades to create ways to reduce carbon emissions and pollution. The Kyoto Protocol and Paris Agreement are two major international environmental agreements.

The 1997 Kyoto Protocol is an international treaty that entered into force in 2005. It committed parties to reducing greenhouse emissions on the recognition of the fact that global warming exists and carbon dioxide emissions are a main cause. Nations participating in this treaty agreed to specific targets. It put much of the burden of reduction on developed nations, on the thinking that they contribute more emissions. The United States never joined this agreement.

The United States did join the 2015 Paris Agreement on Climate Change, another global pact to reduce greenhouse emissions that went into effect in November 2016. It aims to hold the increase in global average temperatures to below 2°C above preindustrial levels (ideally to below 1.5°C) in order to reduce the impacts of climate change. Each member nation decides how best to accomplish this. That means the United States passes its own laws and chooses what to regulate.

As of 2017, many of the world's countries were working hard to reduce emissions and fossil fuel use, replacing them with renewables. Germany, China, and India were all set to exceed the targets they set themselves in the Paris Agreement. International pressure and real concerns at home, such as the high levels of air pollution in New Delhi and Beijing, have persuaded those governments to take real action to protect the environment. That year the Trump administration withdrew the United States from the Paris Agreement, to considerable protest and outcry at home and abroad. Numerous U.S. businesses and individual states declared that they would independently observe the Paris requirements, indicating a widespread agreement on the importance of slowing or stopping climate change before further damage occurs.

# Power

## 8. Where does our power come from?

When you turn on a light or plug in your computer, you probably don't stop to wonder where that electricity is coming from. But you should. Reliable electricity is the result of a very complicated system linking electrical power plants with houses and businesses.

Electricity is a form of energy caused by the presence of electrical charges in atoms—positively charged protons and negatively charged electrons. An electric current is produced when a mass of electrons released from atoms flow along a pathway called an electric circuit. The rate at which electric charges flow through a circuit is called current. Electric power, measured in watts, is the amount of work an electric current can do. Appliances are rated according to the electric power needed to operate them—for example, a 100-watt light bulb needs 100 watts of electrical power. Electrical utilities measure the power they provide in kilowatts.

Electricity comes from businesses known as utilities. Utilities are public companies that provide public services such as water, natural gas, or sewage. Utilities are generally given monopolies over specific areas because it costs a great deal of money to build all the infrastructure to provide these services and because consumers rely on them for basic activities.

A power plant is a facility that generates electricity for use in homes and businesses. Every power plant uses a source of energy to create heat, which turns a turbine, which spins a generator, which converts kinetic energy into electrical energy.

Many turbines are steam turbines, powered by hot steam that makes them spin around. The power to heat the water can come from fossil fuels such as coal, oil, or natural gas; from nuclear reactions; or from renewable energy such as solar or wind. A hydroelectric plant can use water to power its turbines. Gas-powered plants use the heat of natural gas.

The current generated by the turbine can then be sent out along transmission lines into the power grid. First it is sent to a transmission substation, where it is converted into higher voltage and then sent out on long-distance transmission lines. When it reaches its destination, it enters a power substation. There its voltage is stepped down to lower levels usable in homes and sent out onto the distribution grid where it reaches homes, office buildings, factories, and other consumers.

According to the U.S. Energy Information Administration, in 2016, 65 percent of the electricity used in the United States was obtained from burning fossil fuels. Of that, 34 percent was from coal and 30 percent from natural gas. Another 15 percent was from renewable sources; wind and hydropower each accounted for about 6 percent, with small amounts from solar, geothermal, and biomass. Very little electricity was generated from burning petroleum. A significant amount of electricity—about 19 billion kilowatt-hours—was generated by small-scale photovoltaic systems, such as rooftop solar panels.

## 9. What are fossil fuels and why aren't they considered green?

Fossil fuels, including coal, petroleum, and natural gas, are substances that were formed by the decomposition of plants and animals that lived millions of years ago. Coal is a solid. Petroleum, or oil, is a liquid; the fuel sold at gas stations is petroleum. Natural gas is a gas, not a liquid; it is *not* what people put in their cars. Because fossil fuels are made mainly of carbon, they make excellent fuels for the generation of electricity and powering vehicles.

Fossil fuels are not "green," and using them is not sustainable. First, getting fossil fuels out of the ground is environmentally destructive. Second, burning them releases huge amounts of carbon and other substances into the atmosphere, contributing to air pollution and rising global temperatures. Third, fossil fuels are nonrenewable. It took millions of years for them to form, and once they are gone, they cannot be remade.

Most fossil fuels formed from plants and animals that lived during the Carboniferous Period, between 359 and 299 million years ago. (This is long before dinosaurs, which lived between about 252 and 66 million years ago.) The planet was warm, wet, and swampy in those days. When plants died, they sank into the swamp and were covered by wet soil and water. Microscopic organisms called plankton also died and sank to the bottoms of oceans and lakes.

Over the years, soil built up on top of these dead organisms, compressing them. Oxygen could not reach them so they did not rot. Instead, they got hotter and denser as the pressure on top of them increased, and eventually they turned into fossil fuels. Trees and plants turned into peat, which is itself a fossil fuel, and then finally into hard coal. Plankton and algae turned into petroleum, natural gas, and oil shales. The minerals surrounding them compressed into sedimentary rock.

Getting fossil fuels out of the ground is not easy. Coal is removed by mining, which involves digging up large areas or creating underground holes that can collapse. Oil deposits can be far beneath Earth's surface, requiring deep wells. Transporting oil can be risky, and oil spills are devastating to the environment; for example, the Deepwater Horizon spill of 2010 released over 200 million gallons of oil into the Gulf of Mexico, which killed marine animals and damaged ecosystems for many miles around the area. Hydraulic fracking has allowed oil and gas companies to access new deposits of fossil fuels but is creating its own environmental problems, such as increased numbers of earthquakes.

Fossil fuels release their energy through combustion or burning. This is the same process that makes wood or candles burn. Burning breaks the fuels down into their component elements, carbon and hydrogen. These elements form new gases, including carbon dioxide and methane. Both of these are greenhouse gases, which collect in the atmosphere and hold heat near Earth's surface. The more these gases accumulate in the atmosphere, the hotter the planet becomes. The combustion of fossil fuels also emits other pollutants that accumulate in the atmosphere and cause a variety of health problems, including millions of premature deaths every year.

Finally, fossil fuels are nonrenewable. It is easy to see why. It took about 300 million years to form the current supply of oil, gas, and coal. Once they are used up, there will be no more. (Even if we had 300 million years to wait, the conditions that produced our current fossil fuels no longer exist; dead organisms mostly decay now.)

We might be close to using up available supplies of fossil fuels. Demand for fossil fuels from rapidly growing economies is causing the rate of consumption to rise rapidly, which will use up reserves that much faster. Depending on the estimate, oil production might have peaked already, or it might plateau this century and continue steadily for decades. Some sources suggest that oil and natural gas will be effectively gone by the late 21st century and coal in the early 22nd century. Other sources say that reserves are ample, and we can use these fuels as long as we need them—though climate change and air quality might require a change before this happens.

Why do we use fossil fuels? Fossil fuels contain more energy per mass than nearly anything else, so they can produce a large amount of power. This is one reason it has so far been difficult to replace them; other sources of power just haven't been as efficient. In addition, a huge segment of the economy is heavily invested in fossil fuels and has no wish to give up its market share. For those reasons, it is likely that fossil fuels will be with us for many years to come.

## 10. What are emissions?

Emissions are gases and small particles that enter the air through man-made or natural processes. Emissions are a significant source of air pollution and a major contributor to increasing global temperatures.

Any time you see a cloud of smoke, you are seeing emissions enter the air. Of course, you do not see most emissions. Emissions come in different sizes, ranging from invisible gases such as carbon dioxide and sulfur oxides to fairly large particles of carbon and soil.

Emissions come from various sources, including vehicles, industry, and natural processes. When you build a campfire or burn a candle, the smoke that rises from the flames contains emissions. The black smoke that leaves an accelerating car's tailpipe and the clouds of smoke rising from a power plant's smokestack are emissions.

Natural processes create emissions, too. Volcanoes emit great clouds of black smoke and gases that come from beneath Earth's surface. Wind can kick up dust that can travel thousands of miles in the air. Even plants emit chemical compounds that can linger in the air.

Emissions are the main source of air pollution. Greenhouse gas emissions contribute to increased global temperatures. Greenhouse gases such as carbon dioxide and methane trap heat near Earth's surface.

Scientists classify emissions according to their sources. Natural sources of emissions include volcanoes, plants, wind and dust storms, and even cattle, which produce methane through their digestive processes. Human activity, however, produces the majority of emissions. About 80 percent of greenhouse gas emissions come from electricity production, transportation, and industry. The other 20 percent comes from buildings and agriculture. Scientists also break down emissions by whether their sources are stationary or mobile. Stationary sources include factories and power plants. Mobile sources include automobiles, ships, airplanes, and anything else that moves around.

The regulation of emissions is one of the main ways that governments control levels of air pollutants. Vehicle emissions performance standards set thresholds of pollutants that vehicles can produce. The U.S. Environmental Protection Agency (EPA) regulates emissions at the federal level, but individual states can set their own stricter standards if they wish. California sets higher standards than the federal requirements, and several other states follow these rules. Some states require regular emissions testing to ensure that vehicles comply; others make the testing voluntary.

States also set standards to regulate emissions from the generation of electricity. The EPA sets national standards through the Clean Air Act; these standards set thresholds for ozone, carbon monoxide, sulfur dioxide, nitrogen oxides, lead, and particulate matter. If states do not meet these standards, they are expected to produce regulations to ensure that they do. Some states have set their own stricter emissions standards; California has led the way in this area.

Stricter laws are becoming the rule around the world. Industry and auto manufacturers typically protest because it is expensive to redesign their products and machinery, but efficient technology is available. Emissions regulations are a good way to force businesses to improve their products to make them less dangerous to human health.

## 11. What is bad about air pollution?

Air pollution is bad because it makes it hard to breathe, damages lungs and heart, and kills people. It can also kill plants, pollute water, and change the weather.

Air pollution really is deadly. In 2016, the International Energy Agency estimated that polluted air causes some 6.5 million premature deaths each year. This is close to the World Health Organization's 2012 estimate of 7 million deaths caused by air pollution. The American Lung Association actually ranks cities by levels of air pollution. Los Angeles, Fresno, Washington, DC, Atlanta, Pittsburgh, Dallas, and Houston are among the most polluted cities in the United States. Cities in India and China, however, have much worse air. Delhi, India, had 15 times the safe level of particulate pollution in 2014. On bad days, people cannot even leave their houses. People in Beijing, China, sometimes have to wear face masks when they walk outside.

An air pollutant is any substance in the air in sufficient concentrations to harm living organisms. Pollutants can be gases such as carbon monoxide, solids such as ash, or liquids. Amounts matter. Carbon monoxide and sulfur dioxide naturally exist in the air in small concentrations, but they are classified as pollutants when their concentrations become high enough to be harmful. Some pollutants are emitted directly into the air, such as the exhaust from an automobile. Other pollutants form in the air through chemical reactions.

There are several types of air pollutants, most of them produced by motor vehicles, industrial processes, and the production of electricity.

- Carbon monoxide is a colorless, odorless gas that can kill people if they breathe it in a high-enough concentration; because it is in automobile exhaust, a person can die from being in a closed garage with a running car.
- Nitrogen dioxide can cause serious respiratory problems and can turn the air a faint reddish-brown in high-enough concentrations. It is particularly dangerous to people who live near major roads. It can react with water to form acid rain.
- Sulfur dioxide causes respiratory problems and can harm crops. It is also a major contributor to acid rain.
- Ozone is a form of oxygen gas that occurs naturally at high altitudes in the atmosphere but is a pollutant on the ground. It forms when sunlight reacts with other pollutants. It can cause coughing and throat irritation and can contribute to bronchitis and pneumonia.
- Volatile organic compounds (VOCs) are hydrocarbons like fossil fuels that exist as gases in the air. Methane is the best-known VOC; it is a greenhouse gas, holding heat near Earth's surface and contributing to rising global temperatures. Benzene is a carcinogen, a substance that causes cancer. Chlorofluorocarbons destroy the ozone layer.
- Lead is not nearly the pollutant it once was. In the 1970s, lead was added to gasoline to improve engine performance. Lead in human bodies, though, can damage the nervous system, cause permanent learning disabilities. A high-enough concentration can kill a human. By 1999, most developed nations had eliminated all lead in gasoline, and lead levels in the United States are now much lower than they were in the 1980s.
- Particulate matter is particles of solids or liquids suspended in the air. Pollen, dust, and smoke are all forms of particulate matter; they are

often visible to the naked eye. Metals such as iron, copper, and nickel and substances such as asbestos, pesticides, and arsenic are all found in the air, and they can all cause serious health problems.

When pollutants combine with other substances in the air, they can form other types of air pollution. Photochemical smog is a layer of pollution near the ground formed when sunlight reacts with nitrogen oxides and hydrocarbons to form ozone. Photochemical smog looks like a brown haze near the ground. Acid rain is precipitation that is more acidic than normal. It forms when nitrogen oxides and sulfur dioxide react with water in the air to form acids that then fall to the ground with rain.

Pollution can affect the weather in ways other than global warming. Clouds form when water vapor condenses on tiny particles in the air. Pollution increases the number of particles, which can cause increased cloud formation, which causes increased rain. In many areas, weather follows a weekly pattern. The clearest days are at the beginning of the week, after a weekend of low driving has decreased local pollution. Storms are more likely from Thursday through Saturday, as clouds form around the increased pollution.

The air in the United States is much cleaner than it was in the 1970s, just after the first Clean Air Act was passed. Nevertheless, air pollution remains a serious problem, particularly for people with respiratory problems such as asthma, allergies, or lung cancer. The EPA publishes an air quality index that reports on levels of ozone and other air pollutants. This information can help people with breathing problems plan their medications and activities.

## 12. What are some green sources of power?

Green sources of power are fuels that provide energy without the environmental problems of fossil fuels. They are sometimes called alternative energy sources.

Alternative sources of energy include nuclear power, solar power, wind power, water power, and geothermal energy. All of these can be used to generate heat to turn turbines to generate electricity. All of these power sources have pros and cons.

Wind was one of the first forms of power harnessed by humans, and today it is one of the fastest growing. Thousands of years ago people used wind to propel sailboats. The ancient Greeks and Chinese used wind to power machines. The windmill was invented over 1,000 years ago and used to grind grain or pump water. By the early 20th century, farmers were using windmills to generate electricity for local use.

Windmills today are sleek and tall, a far cry from the quaint windmills of the Netherlands. Their light, strong blades can produce large amounts of power; a single large windmill can provide enough electricity to power several thousand houses. A group of windmills is called a wind farm. The United States was the world leader in wind power generation as of 2012, but other nations added windmills rapidly in the 2010s. Windmills now abound on ridges in Europe. Germany, Denmark, and Spain are wind power leaders in Europe. The London Array off the coast of the United Kingdom was one of the largest wind farms in the world when it was completed, though projects in China are expected to be bigger.

Wind energy has drawbacks. The turbines are hazardous to birds. Some projects are held up or canceled because local residents protest that windmills will ruin the landscape. And windmills can generate power only when the wind is blowing. Areas that depend on wind power must generally have a backup plan.

Solar power can sometimes furnish a fallback for wind power, because sunny and windy weather tend not to peak simultaneously. Solar power uses the sun's energy to produce electricity. By 2014, solar energy from photovoltaics was the third-largest source of renewable energy.

Solar power comes either from concentrating the sun's heat and using it to power turbines or from photovoltaic cells, which convert solar energy into electric current.

Silicon photovoltaic cells found in solar panels can absorb sunlight and convert it into electric current. Photovoltaics have long been ideal for small devices such as calculators, but solar panels can now generate enough electricity for serious applications. Solar panels can't generate electricity when the sun is not shining on them, but tracking systems can move them to follow the sun throughout the day.

Water power, or hydropower, uses the movement of water to generate electricity. Water passing through a dam can turn turbines to generate large amounts of power that can be distributed over wide areas. China, Canada, and Brazil make considerable use of hydropower. China's Three Gorges Dam with its capacity of 20,300 megawatts is one of the world's largest hydroelectric power facilities.

The big disadvantage of hydropower is that it requires damming a river, which presents tremendous economic and environmental costs. The United States used a great deal of hydropower in the late 19th and early 20th centuries, but today those old dams have been phased out and new ones are not being built.

Nuclear power comes from the energy released when an atom's nucleus is split. This is called nuclear fission. A nucleus is bound together very tightly, and breaking it releases a vast amount of energy. (The atomic bombs dropped on Hiroshima and Nagasaki during World War II used fission reactions to flatten entire cities.) The reverse process, in which atoms combine to form a larger element, is called nuclear fusion, and it also releases large amounts of energy. Stars, including the sun, produce energy through constant fusion reactions. So far, scientists have only managed to harness nuclear fission, so all nuclear power plants use fission reactions.

A nuclear power plant uses a device called a nuclear reactor to split uranium or plutonium atoms in controlled fission reactions. The heat energy released is captured and used to generate electricity. No fossil fuels are involved, so emissions are low. Nuclear power is clean and cheap, but it is not always safe. Nuclear fuels and nuclear waste are radioactive, which makes them dangerous to humans. Reactors can melt down, which create enormous environmental disasters. The 1986 meltdown at Chernobyl, Ukraine, resulted in health problems and birth defects for decades. The Fukushima Daiichi plant in Japan exploded after an earthquake in 2010, releasing radioactive material widely into the environment. Even a safely operated plant generates dangerous radioactive waste, which must be stored somewhere.

Nuclear power was popular from the 1980s through the 2000s, but today safety concerns have led many nations to phase out nuclear power completely. For example, in 2017, Switzerland voted to phase out nuclear power and replace it with renewable sources. Nevertheless, countries continue to build nuclear power plants. France uses nuclear power for most of its electricity, and China, Russia, and India have been adding new nuclear power plants. In 2015 nearly 20 percent of the power produced in the United States came from nuclear plants.

Geothermal energy uses the natural heat from Earth's interior. Heat from hot springs and volcanoes can be used to heat water and buildings, and the steam can generate electricity by powering turbines. Individual houses can use geothermal heat pumps for heating and cooling. Geothermal energy is available only near the edges of tectonic plates, where volcanic activity is common. It is used primarily in Iceland, Italy, and California.

Ocean tides can also be used to generate energy. The turbines at a tidal station spin when water flows through them. Tidal energy is only an option in areas where there is a large difference between high and low tides, which occurs at a few places in Canada, France, Russia, and China.

Biofuels are another source of power. They are not exactly green because they produce carbon emissions, but they come from organisms that were recently alive and so do not release carbon from deep inside the Earth. Fuels made from plants offset some of the carbon burned because the plants themselves took in carbon to grow. Bioethanol and biodiesel are made from animal and plant products and can generally be used for the same purposes as gasoline and diesel fuel. Biodiesel is made from oils, such as waste cooking oil. Ethanol can be made from various kinds of plant material. Wood itself is a renewable fuel.

Biomass energy has many critics. The European Union, for example, has gotten a large portion of its renewable energy from biofuels. Most of that energy comes from burning wood. Critics claim that the wood is not being sustainably grown and is resulting in deforestation and more carbon emissions than using fossil fuels. They argue that the so-called clean biomass fuel is just greenwashing.

## 13. Can renewable sources produce enough energy to meet our needs?

Many people say that we will never be able to meet the world's electricity needs with renewable sources of energy. The sun doesn't always shine, the wind doesn't always blow, not everyone is situated on top of underground hot springs—and we all need electricity to be available at all times.

But consider this: in February 2017, Denmark generated enough electricity from wind to power the entire country for a day. A power company had just installed new 9-megawatt wind turbines offshore, and along with existing windmills it generated a total of 97 gigawatt-hours—enough to power 10 million European households. In 2015, China wasted enough solar and wind energy to power Beijing for the year. It was generating the power; it just failed to make it to the grid.

That certainly looks promising.

Fossil fuels have a long-standing unfair advantage in the fight to provide energy. As of 2017, developed nations (the G20 nations) provided four times more public financing to fossil fuels than to renewable energy. During the 1990s and 2000s, this entrenched position did put renewables at a disadvantage. Companies selling renewable sources didn't have the money to invest in good technology. They didn't have the existing markets, and they weren't plugged into the power grid.

But times are changing. There are very good reasons for countries to decrease dependence on coal and oil: air pollution, climate change, oil spills, threat of foreign war, money. France has already declared that it will phase out sales of gasoline- and diesel-powered vehicles by 2040. Energy technology is developing rapidly. Smart integration of different sources of renewable energy can prevent gaps in power. A smart grid will let power sources and users communicate with one another so that power is produced and used efficiently.

Alternative fuels are already in serious use in some places. Norway, for example, uses hydroelectric power for almost all its energy needs. It is then free to sell the oil it drills in the North Sea. The city of Oslo is working on producing zero emissions by 2025, building charging stations for electric cars, and using green construction techniques in new buildings. Seoul, Korea, is replacing its bus fleet with new electric buses.

Countries around the world are embracing renewable sources of energy. Costa Rica got 99 percent of its power from hydroelectric, geothermal, solar, and wind power in 2015. Scotland got 97 percent of its power from wind. In 2014, Sweden got two-thirds of its electricity from low-carbon sources. In 2015 it announced plans to become free from fossil fuel and pledged over a billion kronor in support for solar and wind power, energy storage, and a smart grid.

Germany produced 38.2 gigawatts from solar energy in 2014 and was meeting up to 78 percent of daily energy requirements from renewables. Germany isn't even very sunny. Morocco is planning to become a solar energy superpower, exporting electricity generated by giant solar plants around the world. Uruguay gets 95 percent of its power from renewables. China was the world's biggest producer of wind energy in 2014. Kenya gets half its electricity from geothermal energy and another large percentage from wind.

Cities in the United States are following suit. In May 2017, the Atlanta City Council passed a resolution committing the city to generating 100 percent of its electricity through renewable sources by 2035. In 2016, about 17 percent of U.S. energy came from renewables, 15 percent of that from commercial producers and 2 percent from small-scale operations such as solar panels on rooftops. These numbers are on an upward trend; in 2014, the United States was in the fifth place worldwide for solar panels in use and was installing more rapidly. The 21st century seems likely to see some real changes in power generation, thanks to renewables.

## 14. What are some ways to use less electricity at home?

About 30 percent of the electricity used in the United States powers homes. The average household spends over $1,300 per year on electricity. About a third of that power is wasted.

The top energy users are as follows:

1.  Cooling and heating (47%)
2.  Water heaters (14%)
3.  Lighting (13%)
4.  Laundry, especially driers (13%)
5.  Refrigerator (4%)

Heating and cooling are the top energy hogs, using up nearly half the electricity in an average house. Upgrading to more efficient units is one way to improve this, or you could even look into a geothermal heat pump, which uses the consistent temperature of the ground to heat and cool air. If you're not up for the expense of a new system, yearly maintenance can keep your units in good working order.

A good deal of hot or cold air leaks out of the house; sealing windows and ducts can stop this. Insulation in the attic can keep heat from escaping in winter or entering through the roof in summer. A programmable thermostat allows you to set temperatures for particular times of day, so you do not waste lots of electricity heating a home when no one is home. Often air does not circulate well; ceiling fans can circulate both hot and cold air, so the thermostat can be set to a lower or higher temperature without compromising on comfort. Curtains can make a big difference in comfort by keeping sunlight out or holding warm air in. Modern windows or storm windows also help keep air in the house. And clothing is one of the best ways to regulate personal temperature; dress for the weather and you will not have to alter your home climate quite so much.

Water heaters use large amounts of energy because they are always on. American tank-style water heaters keep many gallons of water hot at all times, just in case people want it even though most of the time they don't. In Europe and Asia, many houses use on-demand water heaters that heat water at the moment it is needed; these heaters are available in the United States as well. You can also buy a solar water heater. To keep a tank water heater from sucking up too much power, insulate it and the pipes connected to it to keep in heat. Don't set the thermostat higher than necessary. A drain-water heat recovery system can store heat from used water, saving the energy instead of letting it wash away. And you can always use less hot water—take showers instead of baths, take shorter showers, wash clothes in cold water.

Modern refrigerators are more energy efficient than old ones. Whatever kind you have, make sure the door seals properly so that cold air does not leak out. Don't let the door sit open; grab what you need and close it up again. Some refrigerators have power-saver switches. The Energy Star program certifies appliances that reach specified levels of energy efficiency. Look for that certification when shopping for new appliances.

Lighting can use a great deal of energy. Incandescent light bulbs produce much more heat than light; most of the energy used to run them is wasted. Turn off lights when they are not needed. Motion sensors can turn lights on when people are around and turn them off when they are not. Fluorescent bulbs use far less energy than incandescent. Many municipal utility companies will sell compact fluorescent bulbs for a low price to encourage consumers to use less power.

Small appliances and devices such as computers, ovens, televisions, and dishwashers use less than 10 percent of overall power. Though this does not seem like much, many of these devices are wasteful "vampires" that pull power even when they are turned off. Cable and satellite boxes, televisions, laptops, printers, DVD players, routers, gaming consoles, and microwaves are on all the time. To cut off these vampires, turn them off or unplug them if you can. Energy Star appliances are sometimes built to use less energy when they are on standby mode.

Not all power costs the same. Many utilities vary their prices for electricity depending on the time of day. Daytime power tends to be most expensive because that is when most businesses are open and people are awake. Running power-hungry appliances such as driers or dishwashers at night may cost less than running them in the daytime. Look for rates on peak and off-peak hours on your utility bill to see how this could work.

Solar panels on a roof can save money on power bills—but first you have to get them installed. Installing a 5-kilowatt system on a house cost between $15,000 and $20,000 in 2017, depending on location. Different states offer rebates that can help with this cost, and the federal government offers a tax credit. Some states allow homeowners to sell any excess energy to their local utility in a program sometimes called net metering. Reports from Europe suggest that it takes between two and four years for a household to make up the cost of installing the solar panels. The panels should last about 20–30 years, which makes the installation a good investment. Solar panels also add thousands of dollars to a house's resale value.

Why should you save electricity? Well, of course there is the matter of money—the less electricity you use, the less you pay. But people are funny. Money isn't always the best motivator. A 2015 study found that people who were reminded of the cost of the electricity they were using were much less frugal than those who were told about the pollution impact of their power use. The researchers told this group to think about the toxic gases released into the air from power generation, and this was a much

better motivator than simple economics. It was the most powerful motivator for households with children. Apparently, thinking about poisoning
the air that children breathe was sufficient reason to cut back on power
when money was not.

So there you go—think about how much air pollution you are producing every time you turn on the lights or run your drier. If saving money
isn't incentive enough, keeping the air clean might be.

# Transportation

## 15. How does transportation affect the environment?

Transportation overall is not great for the environment. It uses a huge amount of energy and produces tremendous emissions. According to the U.S Environmental Protection Agency (EPA), in 2014, 26 percent of energy consumption and carbon dioxide emissions came from transportation. Light-duty vehicles, that is, passenger cars, trucks, and sport utility vehicles (SUVs), accounted for 61 percent of transportation emissions. Medium- and heavy-duty trucks accounted for another 23 percent. Aircraft made up 8 percent.

Over 90 percent of the fuel used for transportation comes from petroleum, mainly in the form of gasoline and diesel fuel. Airplanes also use petroleum, in the form of jet fuel based on kerosene or specially modified gasoline.

Trains today are mostly powered by diesel fuel or electricity. Trains accounted for only 2 percent of emissions in the United States, but then the United States does not have much of a passenger train system.

Gasoline and diesel engines are internal combustion engines. They burn a fuel to create heat and pressure that moves pistons that turn a crankshaft. This technology was invented in the mid-1800s. Most engines today are not terribly efficient; they produce more heat than they use to power the engine, and that heat is simply vented. They all produce exhaust gases that are the products of the combustion reaction, in which gasoline reacts with oxygen and releases carbon dioxide, water, and other pollutants. They are all noisy.

A car's engine is often identified as V6 or V8. The number refers to the number of cylinders in the engine. Typically the larger the number, the more powerful the engine and the more fuel it uses, though this varies by model. V6 engines are common in mid-sized cars.

Diesel is a less-refined form of petroleum than gasoline. It is denser than gasoline and contains more energy per volume. Diesel engines are favored for large trucks because they are more reliable than gasoline engines and offer some flexibility; most diesel engines can run on diesel fuel made from vegetable oil, called biodiesel, or even on pure vegetable oil, such as waste vegetable oil from restaurants. Diesel engines are more efficient than gasoline engines, resulting in better fuel economy. A gallon of gasoline produces 8,889 grams of carbon dioxide. A gallon of diesel produces 10,180 grams, but this is offset by the diesel's better fuel economy. Diesel exhaust tends to be black; it is high in other pollutants, especially fine particles (soot) and nitrogen oxides. Ultra-low sulfur diesel burns cleaner than older forms of diesel.

Diesel engines had a moment in the 2000s when manufacturers claimed that their emissions were very low. Environmentally minded drivers in Europe and America bought diesel cars, confident that they were not polluting. Their peace of mind came to an abrupt end in 2015, when the EPA found that Volkswagen had cheated on emissions testing and that during real-world driving the vehicles were producing 40 times their stated nitrogen oxide emissions. Several other automobile manufacturers were found to have gamed their emissions tests as well. The *Guardian* reported in 2017 that at least 38,000 people a year die due to diesel emissions. Most of these are in Europe, where diesel cars were quite popular due to their fuel economy, and in China and India, where trucks produce filthy emissions.

The United States has set goals to reduce greenhouse gas emissions from light- and heavy-duty vehicles by 2025 but has given manufacturers flexibility in determining how to do that. Increased fuel efficiency would be good for the environment while reducing dependency on foreign oil and saving consumers money. The EPA has designed laboratory tests to measure the emissions of vehicles. Every vehicle must be tested to make sure that it meets federal emissions standards. Fuel economy and emissions information on particular vehicles is easy to find online.

A typical passenger vehicle emits 411 grams of carbon dioxide per mile, or 4.7 metric tons of carbon dioxide annually. This is just an average, based on a vehicle with fuel economy of 21.6 miles per gallon driven 11,400 miles. This number varies based on a vehicle's fuel economy, the fuel it uses, and the number of miles driven. A giant SUV that gets 12 miles per gallon is going to produce more emissions than a subcompact that gets 40 miles per gallon. Other tailpipe emissions include small amounts of methane and nitrous oxide. Air conditioners leak hydrofluorocarbons.

The internal combustion engine has dominated car design for 150 years—with cheap oil there was no economic incentive to improve, and it has taken a long time for people to understand the consequences of air pollution and carbon dioxide levels. This is changing now, though. Engineers in the United States and other nations are working on increasing the efficiency of car engines. These range from simply making current technology more efficient, electric accessory drives, new hybrids, engines that can switch from eight to six to four cylinders depending on driving conditions, better fuel cells and hydrogen storage tanks, new batteries, and turbine plug-in hybrid engines for large trucks.

Alternative vehicles include the following:

- Flexible fuel vehicles can run on E85, a mix of 85 percent ethanol and 15 percent gasoline.
- Hybrid vehicles run on two or more types of power, such as a battery and gasoline. Their batteries must eventually be replaced, which is expensive.
- Electric vehicles run on electricity. They must be charged by plugging into an electric outlet. They produce no carbon emissions. As of 2017, there were several models with a range of more than 100 miles, and the field was growing in popularity.
- Plug-in hybrid electric vehicles run on a combination of electricity and gasoline; the driver decides which to use.
- Compressed natural gas vehicles run on natural gas. They must be fueled at special leak-free pumps.
- Fuel cell vehicles are electric cars that run on hydrogen that powers a fuel cell that generates electricity. They emit only water vapor.

Automobile manufacturers are rapidly incorporating alternative vehicles into their fleets. Volvo announced in 2017 that by 2019 all of its cars would be battery powered, either hybrids or entirely electric.

A green vehicle is still a vehicle. It still contributes to traffic and parking problems and it still must be disposed of when it has reached the end of its useful life. Hybrid batteries, for example, contain chemicals that must be contained.

Nevertheless, these new technologies offer some real improvements over gasoline-power internal combustion engines. Electric vehicles do not emit greenhouse gases. Fuel cell vehicles that operate on hydrogen emit water vapor. The emissions from a hybrid electric vehicle vary depending on how it is being powered; if it runs on gasoline, it produces ordinary tailpipe emissions, but when it operates on electricity, it emits none.

## 16. What are some ways to reduce air pollution from transport?

Many cities have been built to facilitate automobile traffic. They have wide, multilane highways with giant intersections. Businesses, schools, and homes are far away from one another, making cars a necessity. The streets are nearly impossible to navigate by bicycle, and giant intersections are nearly impossible to cross on foot. There may be no sidewalks at all.

We all see the consequences. Urban dwellers waste thousands of hours sitting in traffic. Parking is an endless frustration. People don't get much exercise. Air pollution is a deadly problem.

What can be done to improve this situation?

The most popular form of transportation—personal automobiles—is also one of the most costly and least efficient. Cars spend the majority of their time idle, which wastes their capacity and uses up parking. Most cars on the road contain a single person, despite being large enough to hold at least four people and luggage.

The greenest forms of transportation also happen to be the slowest. Walking and bicycling use no external fuels at all. They are great options if you are physically fit and don't have large distances to cover. They are not always feasible in places where roads are designed with only cars in mind, and cycling in particular is dangerous.

Motorcycles and motor scooters use less fuel than cars and take up less space on the road and in parking lots. On the other hand, they are uncomfortable for long distances, expose the rider to weather, can carry only one or two people (although in Asia entire families cram onto small bikes), and can be dangerous.

Public transportation allows a large number of people to share the same vehicles. Subways and buses are ubiquitous in large cities around the world, making it possible to live without cars. Some buses run on natural gas, which produces fewer emissions than gasoline.

The greenest commute is no commute at all. Telecommuting allows people to work at home, communicating with coworkers and employers online. The Internet has made this entirely feasible today.

Ride-sharing is a relatively new option that can maximize the use of vehicles on the roads and eliminate the need for everyone to find a parking space. This can include carpooling, taxis, or ride services such as Uber or Lyft. Some people have found that ride services can entirely take the place of personal vehicles.

Cities have experimented with restricting drivers. Congestion pricing charges drivers a fee to enter a city center. The fee is determined by time of day and congestion level. The highest fees are set for the highest traffic times, in order to discourage drivers from entering at all.

Alternate-day travel or driving restrictions restrict traffic access to vehicles with particular license numbers; for example, odd-numbered vehicles could enter the city on Monday, Wednesday, and Friday, and even-numbered vehicles could enter Tuesday, Thursday, and Saturday. Cities throughout Latin America use this technique, which is fairly effective at reducing air pollution, oil consumption, and traffic. By the late 2010s cities around the world were experimenting with this scheme as severe pollution events called for desperate measures.

High-occupancy vehicle (HOV) lanes are another technique used to improve traffic. Vehicles carrying at least two or three people are allowed to use a special lane that is typically less crowded, allowing a speedier trip. Unfortunately, many cities have recently changed those lanes from HOV lanes to express lanes that drivers must pay to use.

Until recently, many people in the United States really didn't have much choice about transportation. Public transportation is a good, inexpensive option if it exists; unfortunately, many U.S. cities have only minimal public transportation, which makes travel slow and unpredictable, if it is possible at all. Destinations in U.S. cities are too far from one another and roads are too dangerous to make walking or cycling practical. This is why automobiles carrying single individuals—a driver and no passengers—are ubiquitous on U.S. roads.

## 17. Is ethanol green?

Ethanol is a kind of renewable fuel called a biofuel because it is made from organic substances, mainly plant material. Ethanol has been considered a green fuel because it produces lower emissions than gasoline and it does not have to be drilled from the ground like petroleum. The reality is more nuanced, and the benefits are not as clear as was once thought. As of 2014, there were a number of voices calling for the end to corn-based ethanol.

Ethanol is a type of alcohol called ethyl alcohol, which happens to also be the alcohol found in wine, beer, and other alcoholic beverages. It can be made from an assortment of organic materials: corn, sugarcane, grass, wheat straw, and even organic garbage. In the United States most ethanol is made from corn. In Brazil, ethanol is made from bagasse, the fiber left over after the sugar is removed from sugarcane.

Some car engines can run on pure ethanol, but mostly ethanol is mixed with gasoline. Ethanol has slightly less carbon per gallon than gasoline. Since 2007, American refiners have been required to add some ethanol to gasoline as part of an effort to reduce greenhouse emissions. The thinking was that this would improve air pollution and reduce overall carbon footprints because ethanol production requires constant growing of plants, which pull carbon dioxide from the air.

Nearly all the gasoline sold in the United States today contains 10 percent ethanol. All modern gasoline-powered vehicles can handle this. Some flexible fuel vehicles can run on a mix that contains between 51 and 83 percent ethanol, sold as E85. (The mix is adjusted by time of year and location; in cold weather, the mix must have a lower proportion of ethanol for the car to start.)

Supporters of ethanol claim that increasing the number of vehicles using ethanol for fuel could substantially reduce U.S. dependence on oil, especially foreign oil. For example, in 2014, the United States imported 24 percent of its petroleum products. That number would have been 32 percent if gasoline had not been supplemented with ethanol.

How green ethanol really is depends on the entire process of production and delivery. Ideally, ethanol would produce perhaps one-tenth the emissions of gasoline and use up waste plant material besides. In practice, ethanol's carbon footprint varies dramatically, with the least green ethanol producing many more emissions than the same amount of gasoline. The biggest differences come from the biomass used as a feedstock (i.e., the substances used to make the ethanol).

In the United States, most ethanol is made from corn that is specifically grown for the purpose. This requires large amounts of land and other resources, including water, fertilizer, pesticides, herbicides, and fossil fuels. The environmental problems caused by industrial agriculture, which include air pollution, water pollution, and damage to the land itself, destroy some of the putative benefits of producing a green fuel. Shunting corn into ethanol production has had a volatile effect on corn prices. Declines in bee populations might be related to growing corn for ethanol.

Producing ethanol from corn ends up consuming more energy than it produces and emitting more greenhouse gases than would have come from simply burning the same amount of gasoline in vehicles. The Department of Energy has found that for every unit of input used to produce ethanol, 1.4 (or 1.3) units are produced. This is not a great energy balance.

Ethanol is not as efficient a fuel as gasoline. It produces only about two-thirds the power of gasoline, so vehicles are less fuel efficient when they run on ethanol. Critics note that ethanol absorbs water, which can freeze inside pipes and cause them to burst.

Ethanol's emissions are not as clean as supporters hoped. In 2015, scientists discovered that ethanol refineries were emitting much more pollution than had previously been thought. Small amounts of ethanol blended into gasoline do not make much difference in overall carbon emissions. Ethanol itself emits pollutants. Although blending ethanol with gasoline can reduce carbon monoxide emissions, it can increase emissions of volatile organic compounds and nitrogen oxides, which contribute to smog.

Ethanol still has supporters, who claim that it is one key to reducing U.S. dependence on oil and lowering carbon emissions. They advocate that instead of making ethanol out of corn, we use biomass that is not also food, cellulose such as fast-growing grasses or wastes. New technology could maximize the benefits of these materials that otherwise have little value. Cellulosic ethanol has a much better energy balance than corn-based ethanol, with each unit of input resulting in between 2 and 36 units of ethanol. The greenhouse emissions ideally are 90 percent less than gasoline.

## 18. Is air travel ever green? Are there ways to offset the pollution it causes?

Air travel is one of the villains of the environmental movement. Depending on whom you ask, aviation accounts for between 4 and 9 percent of climate emissions. A single round-trip flight between New York and Los Angeles generates 2 or 3 tons worth of carbon dioxide per person. An average American generates about 19 tons of carbon dioxide each year. People who fly regularly generate many times more.

Air travel has been increasing rapidly in recent years, making it the fastest-growing source of greenhouse gas emissions. Twice as many people fly every day now as did in the late 1990s. In July 2015 alone, some 80 million passengers flew in the continental United States.

Airplanes are powered by jet fuel, which is basically kerosene, a refined form of petroleum. Like all petroleum products, it is made mainly of carbon and hydrogen. When jet fuel burns, the carbon binds with oxygen in the air to form carbon dioxide, which is released into the atmosphere. Airplanes also emit nitrous oxides, sulfate, particulate matter, and water vapor. At high altitudes, that water vapor condenses and freezes behind the plane and forms contrails, the streaks of white that crisscross the sky.

Most airplane emissions are produced at high altitudes. This makes a real difference in how they affect the atmosphere. Scientists have found that high-altitude emissions of nitrogen oxides form more ozone than surface emissions. At the same time these emissions destroy methane, another greenhouse gas, but it seems that the ozone load outweighs the methane removal.

Even contrails—the white lines that form behind airplanes as they cross the sky—have an effect on global temperatures. Contrails (the name comes from "condensation trail") are similar to naturally formed clouds, which are also made of water that condenses and freezes in the air. If the air is humid, contrails can spread out and persist for hours, resembling natural cirrus clouds. Like clouds, contrails can trap heat near the Earth, increasing global temperatures. Night flights and winter flights make the biggest difference in warming.

Airplanes are noisy. Noise pollution is a serious problem. People subjected to elevated noise levels—such as those who live near airports—suffer higher rates of heart disease, sleep disturbance, hearing impairment, and general stress. The Federal Aviation Administration has worked on this problem for decades and regularly develops new noise control measures.

The fixes are not easy. Airlines work constantly to make lighter, more fuel-efficient airplanes—fuel efficiency benefits them economically. Jets built in the 2000s are twice as efficient as jets from the 1970s. But designers working with current technology claim that more improvements are unlikely. Some have been experimenting with completely different technology, such as using solar power. Others are testing biofuels. So far, no power source packs anything like the energy per weight that fossil fuels do.

European governments have attempted to use taxation as an incentive for companies to reduce aviation emissions. Under the European Union Emissions Trading System, airlines would have to pay fees for the emissions they generate. U.S. airlines have protested this vigorously, because it would significantly add to the cost of flying and force them to raise ticket prices. Regulating emissions in international airspace has so far been impossible.

How can an individual make a difference? Daytime flight contrails cause less global warming than night flights, though flight time is not always in a passenger's control. Buying economy-class tickets, though it might make for an uncomfortable flight, results in more people using an airplane—which increases carbon efficiency per person. And you can avoid flying unless it is absolutely necessary.

# Waste Reduction, Reuse, and Recycling

### 19. What happens to garbage after it gets picked up?

It's easy not to think about garbage. When you have trash, you toss it in a trash can. If you're in public, you never think about it again. If it's at your house, you have to remember to take your trash out on the right day of the week so that a truck can come from somewhere and haul it away. Depending on the rules where you live, you might have to sort your trash or buy special tags for your garbage bags. But as long as you follow the rules, your garbage simply disappears on a regular basis.

But where is this trash going? What happens to it?

The vast majority of all garbage goes into landfills, also known as dumps. Landfills are holes in the ground filled up with undifferentiated waste. The garbage is compacted and covered with soil on a daily basis. The method is relatively inexpensive because little equipment or labor is required; the garbage goes in the ground and there it stays.

Putting trash in a landfill really is throwing it away. All the resources that went into making the products in the first place—mining metals, manufacturing devices, growing plants and making food, and all the raw materials themselves—are buried in a hole, presumably forever.

About 40 percent of the material in a landfill consists of paper products, and another 20 percent is construction waste. The rest consists of yard waste, food waste, and other things. Disposable diapers account for around 1 percent of landfill space.

The material in a landfill is stored in such a way that it does not biodegrade, that is, break down into its natural components as it would if it were disposed of in a more natural or less-organized way. The garbage is packed too tightly and covered too thoroughly to let in oxygen and water, which are necessary for good rotting. This is intentional, to prevent the landfill from producing greenhouse gases and pollutants that can leach out. As a result, landfills often preserve the objects that are thrown away; food and newspapers thrown away decades ago are still recognizable today.

Landfills present some environmental challenges. Despite watertight designs and efforts to keep oxygen out, pollutants can leach off from the landfill and enter the groundwater, and some organic materials do decompose and emit carbon dioxide and methane, which are greenhouse gases. Landfills in Canada, for example, are responsible for about 20 percent of the country's methane emissions. Because landfills are not meant to be a place for materials to biodegrade, some areas are now restricting the amount of biodegradable material that can be put in landfills. Germany, for example, does not allow any biowaste to enter landfills.

Some areas burn their garbage before sending it to a landfill. An incinerator can reduce garbage to ash, which is much more compact than the original garbage. Advanced facilities use scrubbers to remove pollutants from the smoke before they enter the atmosphere, and many use the heat from the incineration to generate electricity. Incinerators are much more expensive and complicated than landfills, though, which is why not every place uses them.

Most towns and cities pay for garbage collection through property taxes or flat fees. This method of payment makes it very easy for residents to ignore the amount of garbage they generate. As long as the trash fits in the bin, it doesn't matter how much they throw away. Other towns charge by amount, such as by selling ties for garbage bags. This method creates some incentive for people to reduce their trash, but it is still quite inexpensive to dispose of waste.

The world's humans generate a huge amount of garbage. In 2012, scientists estimated that people produced 2.6 trillion tons of waste. About two-thirds of that came from rich, developed nations in North America, Europe, East Asia, and Australia. People in rich nations have generated more and more garbage in recent years, as packaging of consumer products has expanded. The United States, the world's top garbage generator, produced 254 tons of garbage in 2013; China followed with 190 million tons. By 2014, the U.S. figure had climbed to about 258 million tons of garbage, of which about 89 tons was recycled or composted and another

33 million tons was combusted with energy recovery, leaving 136 million tons to be added to landfills. Experts predict that by 2100, annual waste will reach 4 billion tons.

Rich nations regulate their garbage collection and landfills to prevent environmental problems and to encourage the conversion of old dumps into parks or other facilities. Still, finding space for new landfills is becoming a serious problem. But the problem with garbage in North America and Europe is nothing compared to the problems in the developing world.

More than half of the world's people live in places with no regular trash collection. In developing nations, garbage can pile up on the streets, where it is unsightly, smelly, and a health hazard. When it is taken away, it often ends up in illegal dumps where there are no government regulations to control what happens to it. It may be burned, causing air pollution. Pollution can run off from dumps into rivers or groundwater. Very poor people scavenge through dumps, looking for edible food or things to sell but exposing themselves to toxic chemicals and bacteria. Trash increases as a nation urbanizes and adds industry, so Africa and South Asia will be increasing their waste production over the 21st century.

There are many new technologies being developed to further handle waste disposal; these technologies may revolutionize garbage disposal in the future.

## 20. How can I reduce the amount of garbage I produce?

Every bit of "trash" is actually made of resources; paper is made from wood, plastic is made from petroleum, and metal has to be mined and refined. Throwing those things away is a little like throwing away money, with the added problem of environmental pollution.

Solid waste production among Americans peaked in 2000 at 4.74 pounds per person per year and declined slightly over the next years. By 2014, it was down to 4.4 pounds per person, which was still well above the 2.68 pounds per person recorded in 1960.

Food waste is particularly bad. The United States wastes about 30–40 percent of its food supply. This was about 133 billion pounds of food in 2010. This food cost money, water, and energy to produce and transport. Almost all those inputs end up in landfills, where they literally go to waste forever.

There are a number of ways individuals can reduce the amount of waste they produce. This list is just some general suggestions; you can probably think of many other ways to avoid throwing away things that are made of.

1. Consume less. This means buying less stuff, and keep things longer. Don't buy things you don't actually need.
2. Reuse things. For example, keep plastic and paper bags and use them for other purposes.
3. Bring reusable bags to the grocery store. Plastic and paper grocery bags are made from valuable natural resources, and both contribute to the massive garbage problem.
4. Notice packaging. Some food items, for example, are double or triple wrapped. All of that wrapping becomes trash.
5. Use a refillable water bottle or coffee cup.
6. Bring your lunch to school or work instead of buying heavily packaged restaurant or cafeteria food. When you make that lunch, try to assemble it from bulk ingredients instead of individual snack packs.
7. Buy items in bulk packages. (This is cheaper than buying individual packages, too.) Shop from the bulk bins at the grocery store.
8. Look for items made of recycled materials.
9. Try to stop junk mail from coming to your house. Catalogs and fliers use tons of paper.
10. Compost your food waste.
11. Buy clothes at second-hand stores. Give your old clothes to charities or sell them at consignment shops. You can even swap clothes with friends.

Much of this just boils down to paying attention. If you think about the waste you are producing and where it goes, you will see many ways to reduce it.

## 21. How does recycling work?

Recycling takes unwanted materials and turns them into new products. It is an alternative to simply disposing of them as garbage. Recycling is an important part of the EPA's (U.S Environmental Protection Agency) efforts toward sustainable materials management, which tries to use and reuse materials in the most productive and sustainable ways possible.

Recycling has many benefits. It reduces the amount of garbage that is simply buried in landfills. It reuses the materials that went into products, eliminating the need to acquire raw materials—important with items that came from fossil fuels, such as plastics. Reusing materials requires less energy than drilling or mining for new ones, which helps prevent pollution and greenhouse gas emissions.

According to the EPA, in 2014 the United States produced about 258 million tons of municipal solid waste. Only 66 million tons of that was recycled. Another 23 million tons was composted. That rate—34.6 percent of the total garbage recycled or composted—was a huge improvement over levels around the time cities and towns began implementing recycling programs in the mid-1980s, when only 10 percent of garbage was recycled or composted.

Today many cities and towns have municipal curbside recycling. People can place recyclable materials in a special container separate from regular garbage. These materials are collected by a truck and brought to a recovery facility. There they are sorted, cleaned, and repurposed into new materials. High-tech sorting facilities use machines and computers to make quick work of separating materials.

Materials that can be recycled in curbside programs include the following:

1. Paper. Paper can be made into new paper. This is much better than constantly cutting down trees to make paper. About 30 percent of solid waste is paper; about 65 percent of this paper was recycled in 2014.
2. Plastics. Plastics are made from fossil fuels such as petroleum, natural gas, and coal. Plastics come in many different forms, not all of which can be recycled everywhere; the number on the bottom of a plastic container tells you the type of resin it is made of. Out of the 33 million tons of plastics thrown away in 2014, only about 10 percent was recycled.
3. Glass. Glass is made of sand, which is mostly silicon dioxide. It can be recycled repeatedly, and typically recycling it is cheaper than making new glass from raw materials. About 26 percent of the 11.5 million tons of glass waste was recycled in 2014.
4. Aluminum. Scrap aluminum can easily be made into new aluminum products. Recycling aluminum uses about one-twentieth the energy required to mine new aluminum. In addition, aluminum in the environment contributes to acid rain, so it is best to keep aluminum out of landfills.

There is a limit to how many times something can be recycled. Paper, for example, can only be recycled into paper of lower quality than paper made from virgin wood pulp. This makes it less appropriate for some purposes.

After a few rounds of recycling, paper can no longer be recycled at all. (Paper also can't be recycled if it has oil in it, which makes recycling pizza boxes problematic.) On the other hand, aluminum, steel, and glass can be recycled over and over again.

The more materials used in a product, the harder it is to recycle. Pringles potato chip containers, for example, contain bits of metal, plastic, and cardboard lined with foil. Some sports drinks come in plastic bottles enclosed in sleeves made of a different kind of plastic. Spray bottles may be made of recyclable plastic but contain metal springs and different polymers in the spray mechanisms. These are nearly impossible for recycling machines to separate.

Coffee pods are made of combinations of aluminum and plastic, which make them hard to recycle. Coffee cups are lined with oil-based plastic, which makes them unrecyclable as well. Billions of disposable coffee cups and pods end up in the trash every year.

Batteries are a particular problem for garbage collection. Alkaline batteries can be thrown away with household waste, though the heavy metals that go into them could be recycled. These batteries no longer contain mercury, which used to be a hazard for landfills. Rechargeable lithium, lithium ion, zinc air, and lead-acid batteries should all be recycled because the chemicals in them are dangerous for the environment. This usually means taking them in person to a collection facility.

Motor oil and household chemicals such as paints, cleaners, and pesticides are all hazardous to the environment. You should never pour these substances down the drain or put them out with regular trash. Home and garden centers may be able to recycle these items for you. Tires are another problem; most garages will take old tires and recycle them.

Every municipality has its own rules about recycling. Some towns fine residents who do not recycle appropriate items. Others charge consumers a deposit for buying certain items, such as drinks in bottles or cans; when a consumer returns a container, he or she is reimbursed the amount of the deposit. Sometimes a city will abruptly change the list of substances it accepts; for example, it may stop accepting glass. This is because recycling is a commercial business. A recycling facility will accept only the substances it can profitably resell. Breaking even with recycling can be difficult.

## 22. What is the best way to compost food and yard waste?

Between one-third and one-half of garbage in landfills does not need to be there. Yard waste, grass clippings, and vegetable scraps could all be breaking back down into soil, returning their irreplaceable nutrients to the environment. In landfills, all that beautiful organic material goes to waste. Landfills are filling and closing rapidly, so reducing that garbage load is a great way to live green.

Fortunately, there is a way most people can help with this problem. Compost is one of the best ways to reduce garbage and improve the environment at the same time. Compost is simply organic material that has been returned to the soil, where it can do some good.

Organic material is anything that was once alive, including plants and animals. It's called organic because it contains the element carbon. Soil needs organic material to provide nutrients to the things that grow and live in it. In nature, organic material gets into the soil all the time. Leaves fall to the ground, plants die, and animals poop or die themselves. All of those things decay and become part of the soil. The decay is the work of microbes that live in the soil and feed on dead organic material. Bacteria, fungi, and even worms contribute to the breakdown process. This is how nature makes its own organic fertilizer.

When you compost, you save up your kitchen scraps and yard waste and allow it to decay. Then you can put it on your garden, where it will enrich the soil and act as a natural fertilizer.

At its most basic, composting is very easy. You just pile up yard waste and vegetable scraps in a corner of the yard, on top of bare soil, and let natural processes break everything down. It is absolutely not necessary to buy special equipment, if you don't mind waiting months for your finished product. If your main purpose in composting is just to dispose of organic materials without sending them to the landfill, this method works fine.

If you want faster compost, or are simply interested in the science behind the process, though, there are several things you can do to improve your mix.

1. Use a mix of brown and green material. Brown material includes dead leaves, twigs, bark, and even things like shredded newspaper (which is made of wood pulp). These consist mostly of carbon. Green material is green or at least wet: grass clippings, green leaves, vegetable scraps, fruit peelings and cores. Even coffee grounds are considered green. If you are building a pile from scratch, alternate dry browns and wet greens. This mix provides sufficient nitrogen to feed the composting microbes. You can also add egg shells, which contain calcium that plants need.

2. Water the pile. The microbes that break down organic material need water to do their work. Covering the pile to keep it moist can help build heat to speed the reactions.

3. Turn the pile regularly to let air in so the microbes can breathe.
4. Keep the compost hot. Heat keeps the microbes working. A well-composed compost pile will actually generate its own heat, as the microbes give off energy. Placing the compost in the sun will help keep things cooking. If you get fancy, you can use a thermometer to check the temperature of the pile to make sure it stays hot. If it cools off, stir it and add more water.

The compost is ready to use when it is soft and brown and does not look obviously like a pile of scraps or yard waste. How long the compost takes to be finished depends on several factors, including how hot you keep the pile, how regularly you turn it and add material, and your local climate. A fast batch can be done in just a few weeks; a slow batch might take two years.

Plastic compost bins can help speed up the decomposition process by keeping in heat and water. Some fancy versions spin around, tumbling the compost to make the process go faster. Some bins let you add material to the top and pull finished compost from the bottom.

Adding new material to a pile can slow down the eventual decomposition of everything. One way around this problem is to have two piles: one that you add new materials to and another that you just stir and water and wait to finish.

Another technique is no-turn composting. With this method, you layer aerating material such as straw throughout the compost pile. Then you can add new material to the top of the pile and harvest compost from the bottom.

How do you keep a compost pile from looking and smelling like a garbage heap? Avoid the following:

• Meat
• Bones
• Oils and grease

All of those will rot and stink, even though technically they are organic material and will decompose into nice, fertile soil. You just don't want them doing that in your backyard.

It's easy to get into a kitchen composting routine. Get a container with a lid and keep it on the counter or under the sink. Whenever you cut up vegetables or peel fruit, put the scraps in the container. Then every day or so carry the scraps out to your compost pile.

One fun way to make compost, even indoors, is called vermicomposting. This technique uses worms to break down organic material. A worm composting bin is a little more complicated than a regular outdoor bin because it needs to provide air for the worms without letting them escape, and, of course, it requires worms. The U.S. Department of Agriculture provides red wriggler worms through its extension offices.

Fans of compost are often gardeners as well, but you can definitely compost without gardening. Every bit of garbage you keep out of a landfill helps. In 2014, the EPA estimated that 1.94 million tons of food was composted in the United States. Some cities even have municipal composting programs; San Francisco, for example, requires that all residents recycle and compost any reclaimable materials. Composting has gotten more popular recently, but there is still plenty of need for more.

# Food

## 23. Does agriculture harm the environment?

Though the answer to this question depends partly on how agriculture is practiced, the general answer is "yes." Growing crops transforms the landscape in ways that inevitably affect the environment. That transformation can range from minor and local to permanent and large scale. Industrial agriculture as it came to be practiced in the 20th century is particularly costly to the environment. In the United States, the current food system contributes about 30 percent of total greenhouse gas emissions; the majority of that comes from livestock, egg, and dairy production.

There are several types of agriculture. The simplest form uses human labor or animals such as oxen to plow, plant, and harvest. This can be done only on relatively small areas. Industrial agriculture, on the other hand, relies on mechanization to farm very large areas, often with very few human workers. This type of agriculture depends on chemical fertilizers and crops carefully bred or genetically engineered for high productivity.

People started farming about 12,000 years ago. This development, known as the agricultural revolution, made it possible for complex civilizations to grow and so is one reason our lives today are so comfortable. When Europeans first began settling in North America, almost everyone was a farmer—Native Americans and settlers both had to clear land and grow crops to feed everyone. The environmental impacts of agriculture appeared from the start, but they remained on a small scale until industrialization arrived.

Agricultural technology gradually improved throughout history. Innovations such as a rigid collar for oxen and better plows made it easier to plow. Crop rotation and the use of cover crops helped improve soil fertility and made it possible to use the same fields year after year. Plant breeders carefully selected the best crop plants to use for seeds. They also bred animals to emphasize desirable qualities, such as thick wool or rich milk.

The biggest changes in agriculture, however, occurred during the 20th century, in an event also known as the Green Revolution. Between the 1930s and 1960s agricultural production increased dramatically around the world. Scientists at universities developed high-yield strains of grain crops such as rice and wheat. Chemical fertilizers (developed from chemicals used to make bombs and other weapons in wartime) increased yields still further. Pesticides killed insects that had previously attacked crops. Herbicides were developed to selectively kill weeds. This rapid increase in food helped avert famines in India and Africa. Land under cultivation dramatically expanded around the world.

Today, agriculture is extremely high tech. Corporations such as Monsanto constantly engineer new crop seeds with ever better features, such as the ability to resist disease. It takes fewer people than ever to produce enough food to feed the world's population.

But all of this comes at an environmental cost.

About 40 percent of land on Earth is now used for some form of agriculture. Agriculture causes deforestation and loss of wild habitats. Most farming is done by clearing land of wild plants and using the soil to grow crops bred by humans or to feed livestock. The wild landscape provides habitat for plants and animals, and trees naturally absorb carbon from the atmosphere (i.e., they are carbon sinks). Clearing forests and plowing up natural landscapes is one reason for the tremendous loss of biodiversity the world is currently experiencing, with thousands of plant and animal species going extinct.

Soil erosion and degradation is a tremendous environmental problem. It takes soil thousands of years to form naturally. Plowing it up can cause it to blow away or wash away in heavy rains. Cotton culture in South Carolina permanently changed the soil structure of the state when topsoil drained away toward the coast. The Dust Bowl in Oklahoma in the 1930s was the result of poor agricultural practices, and it basically destroyed the agricultural productivity of a good part of the central United States. Desertification is a serious problem in Africa and Asia.

Pollution from fertilizers and pesticides has caused tremendous environmental damage. Fertilizers can run off into rivers and streams, causing algal blooms that suck all the oxygen out of water, killing the plants and animals that live in it. There is a dead zone in the Gulf of Mexico at the mouth of the Mississippi River that was created by huge amounts of fertilizer washing down the river into the Gulf. This damages the fishing and recreation industries as well as the natural biodiversity of the region. Pesticides can kill insects other than the ones that target crops. Herbicides can kill beneficial wild plants as well as weeds.

Agriculture uses immense amounts of water. Irrigation is essential for successful commercial agriculture, but there is often not enough water for all the farmers who want to use it. The Colorado River, for example, supplies almost all of the water to irrigated agriculture in much of the American Southwest. Crops such as alfalfa require particularly large amounts of water. Cities in the region also want to use this water. The river's water supply has dwindled in recent years, leading some people to fear water crises and conflicts over allocation of water resources. Other sources of water are hidden from view. The Ogallala aquifer, for example, lies under the Great Plains from South Dakota to Texas. It supplies nearly one-third of the water used to irrigate U.S. agriculture, and it too is running dry.

There are solutions to all of these problems. Water conservation practices can make existing water supplies go much further than they currently do. No-till agriculture can help preserve soil. Growing plants in greenhouses or in hydroponic systems can save space and avoid the use of soil at all. In many areas, people are already taking steps to make agriculture less damaging to the environment while still producing enough food to feed the world's people.

## 24. What is organic agriculture?

Organic farming is a type of farming that avoids synthetic chemicals. It uses organic fertilizers, biological pest control, and other methods of improving fertility that do not require the chemical and energy inputs of industrial farming. The National Organic Standards Board, an advisory panel to the U.S. Department of Agriculture (USDA), uses this definition: organic farming is "an ecological production management system that promotes and enhances biodiversity, biological cycles, and soil biological activity. It is based on minimal use of off-farm inputs and on management practices that restore, maintain, and enhance ecological harmony." As an alternative to industrial factory farming, organic has become quite popular among people who want to live a sustainable lifestyle.

In the United States and much of the world, organic farms must be certified in order to use the organic label on their produce. In the United States, the USDA inspects farms to ensure that they meet all requirements. This includes ensuring that the farm does not use any chemicals that are not allowed for organic farming, that weeds and pests are managed in an appropriate manner, and that livestock is raised without antibiotics and growth hormones, kept in pastures, and fed certified organic feed.

Organic farming attempts to be sustainable. Many people argue that industrial agriculture is far from sustainable. It requires huge amounts of fossil fuels to power the necessary machinery. The chemicals that go into fertilizers have to be acquired from nature, and the supply of them is not infinite. Phosphorus, for example, comes from mines in just a few places; some experts predict that these phosphorus reserves could be depleted in less than a century. Even those who believe the world has ample phosphorus reserves acknowledge that geopolitics and physical limitations may make it difficult to mine all available phosphorus. Fertilizers are also pollutants. Sustainable agriculture tries to follow natural principles in order to raise crops and livestock without polluting the environment or using up all the Earth's natural resources.

Organic farmers pay particular attention to soil. Almost all plants grow in soil, and soil is the source of the nutrients that help plants grow. Organic farmers rely on compost, crop rotation, and cover crops to maintain soil fertility. Some farmers mix plants and livestock, allowing animals to graze on fields and add their manure to the soil. All of these practices are time-honored ways to keep farmland productive. To keep down weeds, they may use black plastic to cover the soil, a technique that can also keep water from evaporating too quickly.

Though many people believe that organic farmers do not use pesticides, that is not strictly true. They can use natural pesticides such as pyrethrum, which is extracted from chrysanthemums, or rotenone, naturally produced by legume roots. Critics point out that these natural pesticides can be as damaging to the environment as chemical pesticides, and many organic farmers prefer not to use them at all. Integrated pest management uses multiple natural strategies to combat pests, such as using predatory insects to eat undesirable ones. Rotating crops from year to year, planting crops that repel pests, and insect traps can also keep insects down.

Organic farmers do not use genetically engineered plants and animals. Many farmers favor old varieties of crops, sometimes called heirlooms.

Others breed their own local varieties by selecting seeds from their best crops and carefully nurturing them over the years.

Organic farms increase local biodiversity, which is important for the long-term health of the planet. They produce fewer carbon emissions than industrial farms. They preserve old varieties of plants and livestock, some of which are the result of centuries of selective breeding. Some organic farms use traditional farming methods such as plowing with horses and leather harnesses; this helps preserve knowledge that is in danger of disappearing.

Organic farming can be economically profitable. Organic farms tend to produce less than industrial farms, but not much less; organic systems produce about 80–90 percent the yields of synthetic farming. In developing nations organic farms can be even more productive because the materials are more readily available. Around the world, organic farmers tend to make more money than conventional farmers because they can charge higher prices for their produce.

Critics of organic farming say that organic farming cannot produce enough food to feed the world, a problem that will only grow as the world's population does. Some also criticize large-scale commercial organic farms, which, they say, are as environmentally disruptive as industrial farms. Transporting produce thousands of miles to market can also mitigate the environmental value of an organic product.

## 25. Is meat production bad for the environment?

Meat is one of the most environmentally costly foods. This is easy to understand just by applying simple ecology. Plants, also called primary producers, make their food themselves, using sunlight for energy and taking carbon right out of the air. Every animal must eat something, which makes them all consumers. Plant-eating animals are called primary consumers because they eat the plants that formed themselves. Meat-eating animals are called secondary consumers because they eat animals that eat plants. Every step away from plants means that more energy goes into the mix.

Large mammals such as cattle require huge amounts of resources. A cow is a huge creature, between 1,000 and 1,800 pounds, depending on the breed. A herd of cattle needs food and water to power all that growth. Livestock production uses about one-third of the world's freshwater.

Cattle are herbivores, which means they eat plants. In nature, they graze, spending most of their day eating grasses. Industrially raised cattle often do not eat this way. Instead they live in feedlots, where they are fed corn and soybean meal. That food has to be grown on other farms, which consume water, land, pesticides, water, fertilizer, and fossil fuels. The Environmental Working Group (EWG) has estimated that feeding livestock requires 150 million acres of cropland, 167 million pounds of pesticides, and 17 billion pounds of nitrogen fertilizer. A pound of beef takes over 2,000 gallons of water.

Then there are the emissions. Scientists have found that the pollution generated by producing an 8-ounce steak is equivalent to the pollution produced by driving a small car 29 miles. The EWG estimates that beef production generates about 30 pounds of carbon dioxide emissions per pound of meat consumed. Lamb is even worse, but Americans consume much more beef; about one-third of the meat eaten in the United States comes from cattle. Chicken is considerably better in terms of emissions.

Most emissions occur during the production phase, that is, before the meat leaves the feedlot. The process of raising livestock generates emissions from fossil fuel use, but the animals themselves can also add carbon to the atmosphere. Cattle and sheep are ruminants, which means their stomachs ferment plant food to break it down. This process generates methane and nitrous oxide (greenhouse gases that account for about 28 percent of global warming), which they release as intestinal gas (i.e., farts). Methane has 25 times the heat-retaining power of carbon dioxide, so gas from livestock is actually a serious environmental concern. Manure itself generates even more emissions of methane and of nitrous oxide, which are extremely potent greenhouse gases.

What to do with all that manure is another problem. On traditional farms, animal manure is used as fertilizer for crops, but factory farms do only animal husbandry, so they don't have fields to fertilize. Waste is often stored in "lagoons" or sprayed on fields around the CAFO (concentrated animal feeding operation). Runoff from CAFOs is one of the largest sources of pollution in rivers and streams. These pollutants include the antibiotics that are fed to livestock to fatten them up and to prevent illnesses that are common in crowded settings.

Then there are milk and dairy products. Dairy cattle require food and water—lots of food and water. A dairy cow can drink more than 50 gallons of water every day. Producing 1 gallon of milk requires 683 gallons of water. Cheese production generates huge carbon emissions as well, about 15 pounds of carbon dioxide per pound of cheese. This is perhaps half what beef generates but still significant.

Meat production also raises ethical questions. Animals are living creatures that can feel pain. Cattle, sheep, chickens, and other animals all have particular ways of living in nature—behaviors they engage in, foods they eat. Industrially raised animals live in very unnatural conditions. Factory farms, also called CAFOs, crowd large numbers of animals together in areas with no grass and often no natural light.

Cattle raised for meat may spend their first months grazing on pastures, but at about one-year-old they are moved to feedlots, where they are fed mostly corn mixed with antibiotics and other ingredients. This makes them gain weight rapidly. They are slaughtered after six months or so of this diet. Pigs and cattle raised in CAFOs produce vast amounts of sewage waste.

What about eggs? Chickens that produce eggs are kept in battery cages, crowded together and stacked one on top of another. The chickens typically cannot walk, flap their wings, or otherwise do any of the things chickens would like to do. Their beaks are sometimes trimmed to prevent them from pecking one another. Chickens raised for meat are kept in large houses to protect them from predators. These houses are crowded and can smell strongly of ammonia from all the droppings. Their feed may include antibiotics and hormones to make them grow faster.

Animal welfare groups criticize all types of industrial meat farming as inhumane. To begin with, many people believe that animals should not be killed for meat. Animals in factory farms often live in unsanitary conditions. This makes them more likely to catch diseases such as salmonella and E. coli, which can sicken humans. Beak-trimming is thought to be painful for chickens. Cattle are naturally built to eat grass, not corn, and a feedlot diet of corn makes them sick.

If those issues weren't upsetting enough, we also have to consider antibiotics in animal feed. Farmers have fed antibiotics to their livestock since the 1950s. The drugs make the animals grow faster, and they mitigate some of the potential for illness caused by tight surroundings. But this use in animal feed is one of the major causes of antibiotic resistance, which the Centers for Disease Control and Prevention identify as a significant threat to human health.

As the world's people have grown richer, more people in the developing world want to eat meat. Global meat production in 2010 was about 600 billion pounds; experts predict that this amount will double by 2050, with most of this growth occurring in developing nations. Industrial farming, with all its issues, exists to supply humans' growing appetite for meat. Daily, cheap consumption of animal products is probably incompatible with sustainable farming and environmental protection; raising animals on free-range farms is simply too slow and takes up too much space to provide anything like the amount of food required at the price people demand.

There is another solution: we could eat insects. High in protein and other nutrients, insects are popular snacks in Asia and Latin America. All it would take is a small change in tastes!

## 26. Is seafood green?

Fishing is an enormous problem, so huge it is hard to even know how to approach it from a green perspective.

Fishing for wild fish in the oceans is incredibly destructive. Commercial fisheries use huge ships with massive fishing lines or nets that can capture large numbers of marine animals. Because fishing boats are usually targeting just a few types of fish, they throw back the animals they don't want. These animals are called "bycatch," because they are byproducts of the target catch. Giant nets can capture all kinds of animals—dolphins, sea turtles, sharks—all of which get hauled on deck perhaps after hours of being entangled underwater. Dolphins and sea turtles must breathe air, so they can drown before being hauled up. Most of the other animals die before they can be returned to the sea. In addition, giant nets that drag along the bottom of the ocean can destroy the seabed, including coral reefs and all the animals that live among them.

Modern fishing fleets are incredibly good at finding and catching fish, using all modern technology, so the sea creatures really do not stand a chance against them. Ocean fishing is a global problem; all the world's nations share the oceans, so it is very difficult to prevent every fishing boat from breaking rules. Some nations have very energetic fishing fleets. China, for example, added hundreds of massive ships to its fleet just between 2014 and 2016. Its fishing boats regularly travel to the Atlantic waters off the coast of Senegal, where they can easily outcompete the local fishermen. This is just a continuation of a pattern of several centuries standing, in which fishing boats travel long distances to catch desirable fish, and of overfishing that forces them even further afield.

We are actually running out of fish. Targeting one type of fish or shellfish can rapidly deplete populations of that animal. This practice, called overfishing, has resulted in the loss of many kinds of sea creatures. Cod, for example, dropped to 1 percent of its historical levels after years of overfishing. Whaling in the 19th century caused severe drops in populations of many species of whales. Sharks, hunted for their fins and meat, have also had their populations reduced by more than 99 percent. The Food and Agriculture Organization has estimated that some 70 percent of the world's fisheries are depleted or gone.

Fisheries management is one partial solution—the cod fisheries of New England, for example, have been carefully regulated for years—but at the international level it has proven nearly impossible to manage all the world's fishing fleets. Fish are just worth too much money, and people continue to buy them.

Many experts claim it is unreasonable to try to feed the world's human population with wild fish. After all, we don't still hunt wild birds and mammals for food. Fish farming is a possible solution that could be more sustainable. In fish farms, fish are raised in lakes, rivers, or caged areas of the ocean. About half the fish and seafood consumed in 2016 was raised in farms.

Fish farming presents its own environmental problems, though. Salmons, for example, are carnivores; they are fed fishmeal, which comes from fish caught in the wild. The EWG has found that farmed salmon produces emissions equivalent to those of pork or cheese, mainly because people throw away so much more salmon.

Farmed fish suffer the same disease and pollution problems as factory-farmed mammals and birds. Diseases can escape farms and infect wild fish. Pollution from farms can destroy local habitats. Many fish farms are in countries with lax environmental regulations and environmental problems. Shrimp farming in Asia, for example, has been linked to the destruction of wild wetland ecosystems. The World Wildlife Federation and other groups have been working to make fish farming more sustainable and create certification programs to encourage responsible handling of habitats.

So what is the best way to approach seafood consumption while the world works out the problems of fishing and aquaculture? Be an informed consumer, which means doing research. The Marine Stewardship Council (MSC), Aquaculture Stewardship Council, and Monterey Bay Aquarium keep lists of sustainable seafood sources. The MSC, for example, certifies more than 20,000 fish and shellfish as safe to eat. Typically this means smaller fish and shellfish lower on the food chain.

## 27. Are organic foods really better?

Organic foods have become very popular in the United States and countries around the world. People want to know that producing the food they eat is not destroying the environment.

The USDA's National Organic Program certifies foods so that consumers know what they are getting. An organic label may appear on a fruit or vegetable, a carton of milk or eggs, a package of meat, or other single items. A prepared food labeled 100 percent organic is made entirely of organic ingredients. A food labeled simply organic must contain at least 95 percent organic ingredients. "Made with Organic Ingredients" means that the food contains at least 70 percent organic ingredients.

Free-range chickens are given more space to move. Organic chickens are given room and are not fed antibiotics. They grow more slowly and lay fewer eggs, so their eggs and meat cost more, but many people find that a fair price to pay.

Are organic vegetables really better than conventionally grown ones? They certainly contain lower levels of pesticides. Strict rules about using manure as compost mean they probably will not cause food-borne illnesses. Some studies have found that organic vegetables contain more vitamins, minerals, and antioxidants, though the differences are slight.

Organic meat, milk, and eggs contain fewer hormones and antibiotics, and the animals are raised in more natural conditions than conventionally raised livestock. Some experts believe that grass-fed animal products are much healthier for human consumption than meat or milk from animals raised on corn, which is not their natural food.

Unfortunately, the green consumer must be wary of greenwashing. Fraud involving organic products is ubiquitous. The United States imports millions of tons of soybeans, corn, coffee, and other food products from other nations. There have been numerous cases of food arriving in the United States labeled organic but in fact being contaminated with pesticides. Organic products sell for a higher price than ordinary ones, which creates a serious incentive for exporters to mislabel their products. The labeling can happen at any point on the supply chain, too, making it difficult to track.

It may boil down to what concerns you most. If you care about living green and protecting the environment, organic products are probably better than industrial farming—but you will have to do your research.

## 28. Is vegetarianism or veganism the greenest way to eat?

Many people find the environmental and moral issues associated with meat eating insurmountable. They decide not to eat meat at all, choosing to be vegetarian or vegan.

A vegan eats only plant-based products (and fungi, if you include mushrooms). That means no butter, no gelatin (made from animal collagen), no cream or milk in coffee. A vegetarian might be more flexible.

An ovo-lacto-vegetarian, for example, eats plants, eggs, and dairy products. Some people who claim to be vegetarian eat fish and seafood. Some people do not eat the flesh of mammals but will eat chicken, which comes from birds. Some people do not use leather products.

If Americans and other people who eat "Western" diets were to switch to a diet that contained no red or processed meats, greenhouse emissions would be considerably reduced. Animal-based products are responsible for the majority of the carbon emissions produced in U.S. food systems. Compared to growing potatoes or rice, producing beef requires 160 times more land per calorie, and it produces 11 times more greenhouse gases. Vegetable protein sources such as beans, lentils, and tofu produce less than one-tenth the emissions of beef. Millions of people around the world eat a vegetarian or vegan diet for their entire lives; it is possible to be quite healthy without killing or exploiting animals for food.

A study of a large group of vegetarians, the Seventh Day Adventists, found that vegetarian diets produce a third less emissions than nonvegetarian diets. (This study also concluded that vegetarians live longer than meat-eaters.) In fact, researchers at Loma Linda University in 2017 claimed that if Americans switched to legumes (beans) instead of beef, the United States could reach 50–75 percent of its greenhouse gas reduction targets for the year 2020.

British researchers have suggested that the biggest step individuals could make toward lowering their carbon footprints is to eat much less red meat—this could be even more helpful than cutting back on driving. In 2017, University of California scientists found that changing American diets to decrease meat and increase vegetables could make a real difference in environmental impact as well as decreasing obesity and cancer.

On the other hand, critics insist that to make an accurate assessment, all the environmental impacts of a food should be considered. Transporting vegetables vast distances might have more impact than eating beef raised 20 miles from the table. Vegan diets in the United States, at least, can involve some products that are environmentally costly to raise, such as almonds, which are notorious for using large amounts of water. They also point out that not all land can be used equally for agriculture. Grazing land, for example, works well for grazing cattle but not for growing crops. In addition, researchers at several universities and the U.S Environmental Protection Agency (EPA) have questioned some of the emissions numbers associated with livestock, claiming they are much lower than often stated.

Critics of vegetarian and vegan diets also suggest that humans need some animal products in their diet for optimum health. After years of advice to eat a diet low in fat and high in carbohydrates, Americans are plagued with an unprecedented epidemic of obesity and diabetes; eating more saturated fat (from animal foods) and fewer carbohydrates, they say, would go a long way to reducing the national waistline. Of course, most people who gain too much weight are not eating vegan or vegetarian diets full of fresh, unprocessed food.

If you want to reduce your carbon footprint from food but aren't sure you want to be completely vegetarian, you can at least reduce the amount of meat you eat. Beef is the most environmentally costly meat. If you can't live without steak, save it for special occasions.

## 29. Is local food really greener than food from far away?

The food that we eat is often grown very far away from where we eat it. Take a look at the stickers on the fruit in your local grocery store. You will see apples from Chile, bananas from Nicaragua, and tomatoes from Canada. Packaged foods come from factories across the country. That food travels on trucks, trains, ships, and airplanes that crisscross the country and the globe.

Experts have estimated that in the United States, food travels an average of 1,500 miles to reach consumers. A researcher in 2005 found that the ingredients in a carton of strawberry yogurt—milk, sugar, strawberries—traveled over 2,200 miles just to get to the processing plant to be made into yogurt, which still had to be shipped out to stores and consumers. This obviously has to involve costs—money, environmental degradation, and carbon emissions—which has led many to embrace the local food movement.

Local food, farmers' markets, and farm-to-table movements are very popular today. People like the idea of buying food that was raised close to home, and they want to support local farmers. People who eat locally even give themselves a fancy name: "locavores."

Local food in this context is generally considered to originate no more than 100 miles from its point of sale. This is an informal definition, but it generally encompasses an area within easy driving distance. Farmers can pick their produce in the morning and have it in the market by the afternoon.

There are some clear benefits to eating locally. Eating local food usually produces fewer carbon emissions than food that comes from far away. Local food comes from local farmers, often working on a smaller scale than industrial farms, which helps create jobs and preserve farming knowledge. Local farmers often use organic practices, which increase biodiversity and limit harm to the environment. Local farms can produce a more interesting variety of foods than grocery stores. The food is fresher, so there is not as much pressure to sell only varieties that will transport easily.

On the other hand, not every region can produce every type of food year-round. Plants grow only during certain seasons and only in areas with enough sunlight and water. Locavores strive to eat seasonally, consuming only what is available at any given time of year—so no fresh tomatoes or blackberries in January. In regions with long winters, the nongrowing season can be bleak.

The damage caused by transportation is not always perfectly clear-cut. For example, trains produce fewer carbon emissions than trucks, so potatoes that travel 1,000 miles by rail result in the same amount of greenhouse gas emission as potatoes that travel 100 miles by truck. There are other factors to consider. A greenhouse in Maine might be able to produce tasty tomatoes in the winter, but because that greenhouse requires fossil fuels for heating, the carbon footprint of tomatoes transported from Mexico might be smaller. A 2007 study found that growing roses in Kenya and transporting them to England actually produced fewer emissions than growing them in the Netherlands; the artificial light and heat required to grow the flowers in Europe outweighed the transportation costs.

Many university researchers have pondered the question of food transportation as part of food systems. They refer to "food miles," which is the distance food must travel from where it is produced to where it is consumed—farm to table, but on a grand scale. Experts think the best numbers come from tracking greenhouse emissions throughout a food's production. In many cases, perhaps surprisingly, food miles are not the biggest source of greenhouse emissions. Several experts have found that transportation accounts for maybe 10 percent of emissions; the vast majority come from the growing process itself.

Red meat and dairy products are the most costly types of food to produce and transport, and there eating locally may make a real difference. Locally marketed food is often organic as well, and that also is associated with fewer carbon emissions.

So there are several good reasons to eat local food, and it is a fine way to live if you can, but there are also reasons to work to improve the current food distribution system. Increasing the number of trains available to transport food, for example, would go a long way toward reducing emissions because trains are 10 times more efficient than trucks.

## 30. What sort of shopping bag should I use?

Everyone has heard that plastic shopping bags are an environmental disaster. We all know that we should be bringing our own shopping bags with us, sturdy sacks that we can use for years. But is this really true?

In the 1970s, grocery stores put purchases in brown paper bags. In the 1980s, they began introducing thin plastic bags, and by the 1990s consumers were given a choice at checkout: paper or plastic? Environmentally conscious shoppers knew the correct answer: always take paper, which comes from a renewable resource, instead of using plastic bags made from irreplaceable fossil fuels.

But plastic bags took over. By the early 2000s, about 80 percent of bags in grocery and convenience stores in the United States were plastic. And people became concerned that they were an environmental problem. Plastic bags littered city streets and overflowed from garbage cans. They sat in landfills where they did not biodegrade. They found their way into the ocean, where sea turtles swallowed them and they floated in giant garbage gyres. Because grocers did not charge for them, consumers did not appreciate the costs involved and took plastic bags indiscriminately.

All of these things are true, but the solution to the problem has not been simple or obvious.

Perhaps surprisingly, plastic bags were initially intended to be an environment-friendly alternative to paper bags. Instead of cutting down trees, manufacturers could make bags out of ethane, a gas produced in natural gas refining that would otherwise just be burned off. Supporters of the plastic bag industry still point to this use of an otherwise-wasted substance.

Biodegradable plastic may seem like an answer, but the truth is that no plastic bag degrades in a landfill. Actually almost nothing degrades in a landfill, including paper and cotton bags. Paper bags are not really better than plastic, either; manufacturing paper requires more resources than making plastic bags, which are typically made from ethane that would otherwise just be burned off in the refining process.

Some cities and countries have banned plastic bags in an effort to limit litter. Other places have imposed taxes on plastic bags, which typically has the result of encouraging people to carry reusable bags. This does not always work, because the substitute paper bags may generate just as much waste but cost more to make. Many countries and states have started to encourage consumers to recycle plastic bags, bringing them back to the store or at curbside. This is a fairly good solution because it extends the life of the resource and helps reduce the overall number of bags.

The practice of giving customers multiple free plastic bags to hold their grocery purchases is not universal. People do not necessarily assume that they will be given bags for free every time they shop. In stores in Europe and Asia customers are expected to provide their own grocery bags or to pay a small fee to purchase the ones they use. People accustomed to shopping at local farmers' markets habitually bring small string bags with them when they go out.

Many Americans have adopted this practice and bring reusable shopping bags to grocery stores when they do their shopping. Stores now sell cheap tote bags or give tote bags away to customers, and customers are encouraged to bring those bags with them when they shop. Some stores even charge a nominal fee for plastic bags. This is good to a point—if a person has several sturdy bags that he or she uses weekly for many years, then the person probably is benefiting the environment.

The problem experts point to now, however, is that canvas tote bags can actually have a higher environmental impact than plastic bags, depending on how they are used. The difference comes in the resources required to make them. A 2008 study by the UK Environmental Agency found that plastic bags required the fewest resources to manufacture and transport, and they were the cheapest. It also found that many bags were being reused at least once, to hold garbage or kitty litter or dog poop or dirty socks after football practice (though it is hard to imagine second uses for all the bags that end up in houses or on the streets).

Paper bags, on the other hand, would need to be used seven times to get the same ratio of carbon emissions as plastic bags. Tote bags made from recycled plastic would need to be used 26 times to make up for the resources that go into making them. A cotton tote bag would need to be used 327 times—years of use. To make matters worse, reusable plastic tote bags are not recyclable.

This would be fine if people actually did use their reusable tote bags, but studies have found that many of them do not get used. So many stores give them away that people have more than they need, and they end up in the garbage with the plastic bags. Many people prefer to use plastic bags anyway, for convenience or because they don't want to put meat or dirty vegetables in their totes.

The final word is that reusables are best, but only if they are actually reused—and any bag can be reused. If you buy a tote bag to carry home your groceries, you need to use it regularly. If you bring home plastic bags, use them again.

## 31. Could I produce my own food?

Yes, you can.

Of course, how much food you produce depends on many factors—how much space you have, where you live, how much money you want to spend, and how much time you can devote to being your own food supplier. It also depends on how green you want to be.

Growing vegetables is one of the easiest ways to supplement your diet with food of known origin. When you grow your own, you know exactly how the food was raised—what variety of plant it is, what fertilizers and pesticides you used, how much water you used.

Gardening can be very simple. Plants need three main things: air, water, and light. Air is not a problem because it is everywhere. Plants take carbon dioxide from air to make their own sugars (plants actually build themselves out of air). Water is necessary for photosynthesis and for moving sugars and nutrients around the plant. Light provides the power for photosynthesis.

Along with those main requirements, plants also need nutrients, especially nitrogen, phosphorus, and potassium. You can buy these in commercially produced fertilizer, or you can make your own compost.

Then it is just a matter of deciding where to put the plants. There are many options. Some gardeners put plants in the ground, either straight in the soil or in raised beds. It is often easier to put plants in pots—they may grow better, and you can move them around to maximize sunlight. A greenhouse is expensive but allows people to grow plants out of season.

Light is often the biggest problem for urban gardeners. Vegetables like tomatoes and beans really want six or eight hours of full sunlight; if they don't get that, they won't grow well and they won't set much fruit. People who grow plants indoors or in greenhouses often use fluorescent lights to propel photosynthesis. Different plants require different amounts of heat. Almost nothing grows in cold weather, but very hot weather can also shut down growth.

Choosing plant varieties is one of the most exciting aspects of vegetable gardening. Your local garden center probably sells just a few types of seedlings that are already started, and these can be very convenient, but seeds offer the opportunity to try out different types. Heirlooms are varieties of vegetables that were historically grown but are not currently commercially popular; they often have a very good flavor and are well worth trying.

If you really embrace urban gardening, you might even raise chickens. Not every city allows this, so check before you buy chicks. Raising chickens is a fun way to get fresh eggs, and the chickens produce natural fertilizer for your plants.

Is home gardening really green? Not necessarily. If a garden requires dozens of car trips to the garden center and pounds of fertilizer and pesticides, to say nothing of municipal water, it might cost more in carbon emissions than it saves. But a garden filled with home-produced compost and watered by rain and water caught in a rain barrel, filled with plants grown from saved seeds, at least has some claim to being green.

And it is almost certainly worth experiencing what food production is really like. One lesson most home gardeners learn is that it can be surprisingly difficult to produce much food in a backyard. Plants don't always grow well. Animals steal the vegetables. An unexpected freeze can destroy an entire garden in one night. Gardeners often joke that the tomatoes they raise cost them $10 apiece.

Gardening can take years to master. Good gardeners see it as a long-term project—they get to know the seasonal light and temperature patterns, they try different plant varieties to see what grows best, they learn how to rotate their crops to minimize disease. They really have to see nature in action and fit their own projects into that reality—and that is green living.

## 32. Can restaurant food be green?

Running a restaurant is complicated. A restaurant has to keep food supplies on hand to make any dish a customer orders off the menu, but it is impossible to predict how much food will be consumed. Consumers often do not eat everything on their plates. They may send back dishes they don't like. The result is lots of wasted food.

A survey from 2013 found that this waste amounted to a loss of nearly 16 percent of total food, or 3.3 pounds of waste per $1,000 of revenue. Almost all wasted restaurant food ends up in landfills. About 84 percent is simply thrown away. Another 14 percent is recycled, mostly as reclaimed cooking oil. A tiny portion is donated to food banks and soup kitchens. The reasons for this are mainly practical—it is simply impossible to store and transport fresh food in ways that go beyond the restaurant's daily work.

Many restaurant owners would like to compost or donate their uneaten food, but it is difficult or impossible to do in practice. Small restaurants, for example, do not produce enough waste for a commercial composting company to come haul away their wasted food.

In addition, restaurants use vast amounts of water and can produce large amounts of garbage, particularly if they use a lot of packaging, as do fast-food restaurants. Think of all the paper cups, plastic and cardboard boxes, straws, wrappers, and napkins that are involved in an average fast-food meal. Americans use some 100 million plastic utensils every day, along with hundreds of millions of straws and paper coffee cups and lids. All of that goes to waste. (A UK waste disposal company has called for a tax on plastic drinking straws, which it calls incredibly wasteful and impossible to recycle.)

Fast food is particularly costly to the environment. Fast-food packaging makes up a significant portion of the garbage that ends up in landfills. Studies have shown that fast-food packaging comprises 40 or 50 percent of the litter on the streets. Many of these items could be recycled but are not. To make matters worse, scientists in 2017 discovered that many wrappers and containers leach toxic chemicals that can cause birth defects, increase the risk of cancer, and cause other serious health problems. In Europe and Canada, food manufacturers are responsible for the packaging they use to contain their products, but U.S. manufacturers have resisted any efforts to make them accountable.

In addition, fast-food companies are some of the biggest consumers of factory-farmed meat, which are major consumers of resources and polluters of the environment. Philosophically, fast food contributes to consumers' belief that food should be cheap and available everywhere at any time and require no more cleanup than tossing a bag of paper and plastic into a nearby garbage can. From a health perspective, giant sodas washing down French fries and large burgers is one of the contributors to the current epidemic of obesity.

So what can restaurants do to improve their environmental profile? Donating food to charities sounds like a great idea, and there is a real need for food in many poverty-stricken communities. Restaurants worry about liability, though; they do not want to be accused of causing food poisoning by donating yesterday's unused food. Federal law protects businesses that donate to charities, and sell-by dates are just meant to mark optimum freshness, not the date on which food goes bad. Food can still be donated just after its sell-by date.

In 2013 the USDA and the EPA launched a program called the U.S. Food Waste Challenge, intended to help educate consumers and businesses about food waste and to help them determine the best ways to limit waste through reduction, recycling, and recovery. This program provides software and apps that can help restaurants organize their purchases and usage. Just-in-time ordering and delivery allows restaurant managers to buy only what they will need.

Small restaurants in the same neighborhood can band together to sign composting contracts, which makes composting more economical for them all and makes the composting pickup more efficient.

Restaurant serving sizes inevitably result in waste. Many restaurants serve far more than a single person could (or should) eat for one meal. Some customers bring their leftovers home (in foam or plastic containers that can become garbage, and where the food may be wasted anyway), but a substantial portion is simply thrown away by the dishwashers in restaurant kitchens. Smaller portion sizes could go a long way toward eliminating this type of waste, but many restaurants and consumers are convinced that large servings are necessary to convince customers that they are getting a good deal.

Limiting menu options would allow restaurants to store less food in order to meet daily cooking needs. Efficient packing and storage techniques such as vacuum-sealing meat can keep food good much longer than inefficient methods.

The National Restaurant Association has joined forces with the Food Waste Reduction Alliance, another organization devoted to ending food waste in restaurants and grocery stores. They focus on increasing donations of uneaten food and recycling food waste to keep it out of landfills.

The Green Restaurant Association (GRA) provides guidance for restaurants that want to go green, and it certifies restaurants according to their green practices. It assesses them based on the following:

- Water efficiency
- Waste reduction and recycling
- Sustainable building materials
- Sustainable food
- Energy use
- Use of reusable or environmentally sustainable disposable material
- Chemical and pollution reduction

The GRA's website has a searchable list of restaurants that have met its standards and are certified green. It also publishes a list of restaurant products that it endorses.

And where should a green consumer eat? The healthiest and cheapest option, which is also the greenest, is to limit your consumption of restaurant food. Cook at home and bring your own lunch and snacks when you go out.

But when you do eat out, pay attention. Find a restaurant that is certified green. Use portion control—order only what you can eat. Share an entrée with someone else. Carry a reusable coffee mug instead of getting new paper ones every time you buy coffee. Don't take plastic straws or cutlery if you don't need them. Sometimes you may not have any choice, but at least try to be aware of the impact of your actions.

# Water

## 33. Do I really need to worry about water?

Yes. Water is one of the few things you really do need in life, and though it seems to be everywhere and free, there is really surprisingly little of it. Humans need to worry about two big concerns: depletion and pollution.

Most of the water on Earth—about 97 percent—is in the oceans. Most of the rest of the planet's water is in polar ice caps. That water is fresh, not salty, but not exactly accessible. That leaves about 1 percent of Earth's water as accessible freshwater.

Humans need freshwater to live, so do all land animals and plants. Water is constantly moving around the planet in a process called the hydrologic cycle, or water cycle. Water evaporates from oceans, soil, plants, lakes, and rivers, and enters the air as water vapor. About 90 percent of the water that enters the atmosphere as clouds comes from oceans. It falls from the air as rain, snow, or other types of precipitation. This water can run into bodies of water such as lakes or streams or down into the ground, where it fills underground bodies of water.

All our municipal water supplies come from freshwater sources, such as rivers, lakes, and groundwater. Groundwater, water found underground, is a major part of our freshwater supply. Much of it is in aquifers, underground layers of sand or rock that hold water. People get at groundwater by digging wells; about half of the drinking water in the United States comes from aquifers.

All of these sources are under pressure from many users, and all of them can be contaminated by pollution. The United Nations has found that water use is growing twice as fast as human populations. By 2025, nearly 2 billion people will live in areas where freshwater is in short supply. This is complicated by a patchwork of water use laws that set people up for conflict.

For example, in the United States the Ogallala aquifer runs from South Dakota to Texas and supplies water to much of the Midwest, including thousands of acres of farmland. The Ogallala aquifer contains water from ice that melted after the most recent glacial period, about 15,000 years ago. It has been depleted by decades of agricultural and urban use, as well as use by the oil and gas industry. There is no possibility of rain replenishing it at the current rates of use. By 2016, wells were running dry. Some farmers are switching to dryland farming, without irrigation, but many have no idea what they will do when the water is completely gone.

Droughts are becoming more common in the United States as pressure on water supplies increases. The National Integrated Drought Information System at Drought.gov publishes current drought conditions and forecasts for the future.

Then there is the matter of water pollution. Water pollution can make water undrinkable, kill animals and plants that live in water, and cause the rapid growth of algae.

Every time it rains, water runs off the ground into streams and rivers; if it runs off farmland, it brings fertilizer and pesticides into the water supply. Industrial plants have an unfortunate history of dumping waste products straight into rivers. In many places sewage either drains into freshwater sources or leaches into them accidentally.

Polluted water makes people sick. Cholera, vibriosis, typhoid, polio, amoebiasis, giardiasis, dysentery, and hepatitis A all come from microscopic pathogens that get into water, particularly water contaminated by human feces. Drinking water affected by an algal bloom can cause stomach and liver illness, rashes, neurological problems, and respiratory problems. Disinfectants can be contaminated with dioxins, which can cause cancer. Mosquitoes breed in standing water. Poor waste and water management that allows water to stand in puddles or containers contributes to malaria and other mosquito-borne diseases by creating areas where mosquitoes can easily lay eggs that will hatch and grow into thriving adult insects. Water contaminated with nitrates from fertilizers can affect oxygen in blood; babies can get blue baby syndrome, which causes blue-tinted skin and shortness of breath and can kill.

Sewage has been polluting water sources since humans started living together in cities. Chemical pollution is the result of industrialization and the rapid increase in use of fossil fuels for energy, which began with the Industrial Revolution of the 19th century. By the mid-1900s, water and air pollution were noticeable problems in U.S. cities. The Cuyahoga River in Cleveland, Ohio, became so polluted from industry that it caught on fire several times between 1936 and 1969.

Events like that are what spurred the U.S. Congress to pass the Clean Water Act and Safe Water Drinking Act, federal laws administered by the U.S Environmental Protection Agency (EPA). The Clean Water Act allows the EPA to regulate contaminants such as arsenic, lead, and microbes. Water supply systems are inspected regularly. Other laws and regulations protect groundwater from contamination. Occasionally the EPA or a state agency declares a water source too contaminated for human use.

The Safe Drinking Water Act protects public drinking water supplies. The website lists acceptable levels of contaminants, which include microorganisms, disinfectants, inorganic and organic chemicals, and radioactive particles. All of these contaminants can cause disease in humans, but at low levels these are not terribly dangerous.

Water pipes are a surprising source of pollution. In 2014, the residents of Flint, Michigan, started pulling drinking water from the Flint River instead of paying Detroit for municipal water. The river water was slightly acidic, which corroded the city's pipes, releasing lead into the water supply and into peoples' houses. In 2017, the EPA was working on ways to better protect populations affected by lead. Thousands of cities in the United States have old lead and iron pipes that place residents at risk of lead in their water.

Water pollution is a systemic problem with a huge number of sources. Individual consumers can avoid contributing to water pollution by limiting their use of fertilizers and pesticides. At home, water filters can remove a number of pollutants from the water that comes out of the sink or shower head. Filtered pitchers are a good way to keep drinking water in the refrigerator.

## 34. How can I use less water?

Though it may seem that water is cheap and readily available, this in fact is not true. Water stress is increasing in the United States, including in some areas that seem lush and humid, such as the Southeast. People in California are very familiar with water conservation strategies, but these are becoming important everywhere as water supplies dwindle while more consumers want to use them. In 2014, 40 U.S. states reported that they expected water shortages within the next decade—shortages not caused by droughts but by human use.

The majority of freshwater used in the United States goes to industry and agriculture. In 2010, 45 percent of freshwater was used to generate electricity. Another 32 percent went to irrigation.

The public water supply—pipes that go into buildings including homes and businesses—accounts for about 12 percent of water use. Businesses use about 17 percent of that water. Hotels, restaurants, hospitals, schools, factories, and government offices all consume large amounts of water, largely in restrooms, laundries, and kitchens.

According to the EPA, the average U.S. household uses about 300 gallons of water every day. About 24 percent of that water goes to flushing toilets; another 20 percent goes to showers, and another 19 percent to sinks. Leaks use up 12 percent. Washing machines and other uses make up the rest.

The EPA's WaterSense program is designed to help consumers and businesses find ways to conserve water. WaterSense-labeled products are certified to use less water and energy than regular devices. The EPA also recommends certain strategies to encourage communities to save water. These include accounting for water use, pricing water to reflect its value and scarcity, and fixing leaks to prevent waste. At home, more-efficient appliances and water-saving practices could save a great deal of water.

Water-saving techniques include the following:

- Check for leaks. Faucets, pipes, and toilets can all leak, and little leaks can add up. A water meter or a suspiciously high water bill can tell you if something is amiss; finding the leak is sometimes more challenging.
- Never use the toilet as a trash can. Seriously.
- Get an ultra-low flush toilet. Or put a tank bank in your older toilet to reduce the volume dumped with each flush. A tank bank is a plastic bag you fill with water and hang inside the tank to take up some of the space that fills with water after every flush. A plastic bottle filled with water works well too.
- Take shorter showers. A four-minute shower uses 20–40 gallons of water. You can even do a navy shower—get wet all over, and then turn the shower off while you soap up. This gives the shampoo and soap longer to do their job anyway. (This works well only if your shower will produce hot water after being turned off—some will have a blip of cold.) This is common practice in areas where water is in short supply.

- Install water-saving showerheads.
- Don't run the sink while you brush your teeth.
- Don't use a garbage disposal too much. It requires water to work well, and most of what you put down it could be composted.
- When you wash the car, fill a bucket with water and use that to scrub. Use the hose to wet the car and rinse it, and turn it off in between. Or find a car wash that recycles its wash water.

Washing dishes uses a lot of water, but believe it or not, hand washing is much worse than using a dishwasher. Hand washing dishes can use almost eight times as much water as a high-efficiency dishwasher. Energy Star–certified dishwashers use about 4–6 gallons of water per load and less than half the energy (to heat the water). To maximize efficiency, don't rinse your dishes before you put them in (you can scrape off big chunks of food) and only run full loads.

If you hand wash dishes, fill the sink with soapy water and use that to wash instead of washing everything in running water. If you have a double sink, put soapy water in one side and rinse water in the other. Or don't rinse; people in Europe often just let the dishes dry with the soapy water on them.

About 30 percent of household water use goes to lawns and gardens, and some to swimming pools. This percentage tends to be higher in dry areas, especially where people grow grass and other plants that require large amounts of water.

To save water in the garden, use plants appropriate for your climate. If you live in a dry place, don't plant things that need lots of water. Hydrangeas, for example, don't belong in the desert. Other water-saving tips include the following:

- Water plants early in the day. Water deeply and infrequently; this encourages plants to grow deep roots and makes them better able to resist dry periods.
- Water only when plants need water. Check to see if the soil is dry.
- Water the soil, not the sidewalk or driveway.
- Monitor your automatic sprinkler system. Don't let it run in the middle of a rainstorm.
- Don't grow plants that need lots of water, such as hydrangeas. Native plants are often a good choice.
- Mulch your plants to hold water in the soil. Add organic material, especially material from your compost bin.
- Get a rain barrel and put it under your downspouts. Use this to water your plants.

## 35. How can I make my laundry less environmentally costly?

Laundry is not green. Washing clothes uses water and power to turn a washing machine drum or to heat washing water. Driers use vast amounts of electricity. If you want to reduce your carbon footprint, reducing laundry is a great place to start.

There are several ways to make laundry greener.

- Use an energy-efficient modern front-loading washer.
- Wash clothes in cold water, not warm or hot.
- Wash clothes only when they are actually dirty or smell bad.
- Run only full loads of wash, or make sure to select size of load.
- Hang clothes to dry.
- Iron only when absolutely necessary.
- Avoid dry cleaning, which uses many chemicals. Many dry-clean-only garments can be hand-washed.

The average U.S. household does about 300 loads of laundry a year. A full-sized washer uses somewhere between 13 and 40 gallons per load, depending on how old it is, how large it is, and how efficiently it works. A front-loading Energy Star–certified machine might use just 13 gallons, whereas a top-loader built in the 1990s might use 40 gallons to wash the same load.

The Energy Star program certifies appliances that meet certain standards of efficiency. Older washers, especially those built before 2003, are much less efficient than newer ones. Top-loading washers use the most water because they fill the entire tank with water and submerge the clothing in it. Rinsing is done by draining the wash water and refilling the tub with clean water.

Modern front-loading washers use much less water. Instead of submerging clothes in a tank, they flip the garments around in a stream of water. Rinsing is done the same way, by spraying the clothes with high-pressure water instead of soaking. High-tech washers have sensors that can detect the amount of clothing in a washer and modify water accordingly.

Energy Star has estimated that in the late 2010s, there were still 76 million top-loading washers in the country, one-third of them over 10 years old. Inefficient washing machines cost nearly $3 billion per year in water and energy. An individual modern washer could use 7,000 fewer gallons of water each year than an older model.

Running the moving parts of a washer does not use that much electricity. If you wash clothes in warm water, 90 percent of the electricity used goes to heating the water. Detergent is very efficient at getting clothes clean. Most detergents work very well in cold water, rendering hot water unnecessary for almost all home laundry purposes. Some detergents are specially formulated to work in cold water. Experts have estimated that heating laundry water releases 34 million tons of carbon emissions.

Of course, there is the problem of water pollution. Detergents, fabric softeners, scent boosters, and bleach drain out of the washing machine and into the sewage system, unless they leak out of the pipes and go straight into the environment. Laundry detergents contain substances such as sodium triphosphate, which can cause algae blooms in water. The surfactants that help water penetrate garment fibers do not break down completely during sewage treatment. And chemicals are not the only substances that go from washing machines into the water supply.

Clothes themselves produce pollutants. A study in 2016 reported that a single load of laundry releases over 700,000 microscopic particles. Many of these particles are microplastics, as small as 0.355 millimeter, that come from synthetic fabrics. Polyester and acrylic produced the most. These tiny particles wash down the drain and enter the water supply. Microscopic plastics in aquatic environments are known to be a problem. Baby fish love to eat the microbeads found in exfoliants, and plastics easily absorb liquid toxins that are in the water. Scientists don't yet know the exact environmental implications of microscopic laundry fibers, but they can't be good. (If you want to keep these fibers out of the water, mesh bags can filter them out, and washer manufacturers are developing microfiber filters for washing machines.)

Driers use incredible amounts of energy, so much so that people in many parts of the world never use them. Driers produce about 700 pounds of carbon emissions per household each year. Powering a drier costs about $300 per year. Driers use hot air to get clothes dry quickly. The hot air is vented to the outside. Some models have moisture sensors that turn them off when the clothes are dry, so that they don't spin any longer than necessary.

Until recently it was difficult to design an efficient clothes drier. In the past few years, though, there have been new innovations in drier technology. The heat pump drier, already popular in Europe, doesn't vent the hot air out of the machine. Instead, it runs the air through a heat pump that condenses the water and recirculates the air back into the drier. The drying temperature is lower, so it does not heat up the laundry room as much. The machines are about 50 percent more energy efficient than conventional driers.

To be really green, though, there is always the old-fashioned tech-nique of air drying. This is still the norm in much of the world, including Europe. Many clothes last the longest if they are hung to dry anyway. A clothesline in the open air or a drying rack indoors simply let water evaporate from the clothes. Air drying produces no emissions and costs nothing (though drying racks and clotheslines do cost money). Draw-backs are that air drying requires a good deal of space, and air drying can take a very long time if the weather is cloudy, humid, or cold. Air drying works best in a dry climate with good sunlight and a nice breeze.

## Other Issues and Concerns

### 36. What does it mean that a product is certified "green"?

"Green" is a term that is tossed around seemingly at random, along with words like "eco-friendly," "sustainable," "biodegradable," or "natural." Most consumers would like to assume that a green product has less environmental impact or less potential danger to human health than a nongreen product. It might be made in an energy-efficient manner, in a process that does not emit toxic chemicals as waste. It might be made from recycled material, or from locally grown or produced materials. It could be biodegradable. The truth is that, in many cases, it doesn't mean anything in particular.

You may see the following terms:

- Certified organic: the ingredients of the product are all organically grown—without chemicals or pesticides that can damage the environment.
- Eco-friendly: it suggests that a product is not harmful to the environment but does not specifically mean anything.
- Green: it does not necessarily mean anything.
- Green Seal certified: a product has met all of the requirements of the environmental certification organization Green Seal.
- Natural, or 100 percent natural: the product contains no artificial ingredients and involves minimal processing; must meet USDA standards.

- Made from recycled materials: at least some of the components are recycled.
- Sustainable: it suggests that a product's manufacturer does no long-term damage to the environment but could mean anything.
- Vegan: no animal products are involved in making a product.

Some of these terms do have real meanings. Certified organic or Green Seal–certified products have passed a number of tests. Others are just advertising, used to tempt consumers who are attracted to the fantasy of lowering their environmental impact. This is known as greenwashing, and it can be dishonest but harmless, but it can sometimes cause harm. A study published in 2015 found that many common consumer products advertised as green or organic actually emitted volatile organic compounds classified as air pollutants.

Of course, many products advertised as green really are more environmentally friendly. There are thousands of products that are made in sustainable ways and with natural ingredients and nontoxic materials and that are biodegradable. The challenge is identifying them.

One thing to look for is Green Seal certification. This certification ensures that a product meets the Green Seal organization's Green Seal Standards, which are published for a range of products, including personal care products, household products, paints and building materials, restaurants and food services, and hotels. The standards are very strict and cover a range of areas from sourcing of materials to instructing consumers on how to dispose of packaging.

For example, the GS-50 certification for personal care and cosmetic products states that these products must not include carcinogens, reproductive toxins, and endocrine disrupters or cause eye or skin irritation. They must not be tested on animals. Nanoparticles are limited. The process of making the product must follow strict standards on water use, energy use, and waste and emissions. The production must meet certain social responsibility requirements. Packaging must contain some recycled material and no heavy metals, phthalates, or bisphenol A. Any claims of natural ingredients must be supported with documentation. The label must contain disposal instructions.

The Federal Trade Commission (FTC) publishes Green Guides to help manufacturers and consumers use the same language. These guides try to keep marketers from making broad claims that products are "eco-friendly" or "environmentally friendly" because consumers mistakenly assume that these terms actually mean the products have significant environmental benefits. Manufacturers are advised not to advertise products as biodegradable unless they will completely break down and return to nature within a year, and this term should never be used for items destined for landfills. The guides explain how to write about carbon offsets and claims involving nontoxic or renewable ingredients and renewable energy. The FTC does not get into the details of the terms "sustainable," "natural," or "organic." The FTC has actually sued companies over misleading claims about environmental certification or recyclability in an effort to ensure that environmental marketing is truthful.

There are many other guides to green products. *National Geographic* publishes numerous guides to green living. It may take a little time to research all the products you use, but there is good information out there.

## 37. Should I worry about indoor air pollution?

When you think of air pollution, you probably envision exhaust from cars and smoke from factories filling the air outdoors. Staying inside is one way to escape. But you may not be safe from air pollution indoors either. Poor interior air quality is very common and can have a real impact on health.

Indoor air pollution can come from many sources. These include the following:

- Carpets and flooring
- Upholstery
- Insulation
- Cabinetry and furniture made of pressed wood
- Household cleaning products
- Tobacco smoke
- Air fresheners
- Gas stoves
- Heating and cooling systems

It's a little disturbing to think that the walls, carpet, and furniture in your house might be toxic. Indoor air pollution causes a range of ailments, including irritation of the eyes and nose, fatigue, dizziness, headaches, and aggravation of asthma.

Long-term exposure to indoor pollutants can cause serious chronic illness. Asbestos is a type of fibrous mineral that was commonly used in building materials in the 19th and 20th centuries. Asbestos has fire-retardant properties, which made it useful for building and electrical insulation. Unfortunately, breathing asbestos fibers for decades is very dangerous. People exposed to asbestos for many years can develop lung diseases such as asbestosis, lung cancer, or another cancer called mesothelioma. Asbestos is now banned in most countries, but it has harmed many thousands of people and it is still in many old buildings.

Many chemicals act as indoor air pollutants. Formaldehyde is found in particle board, plywood, synthetic fabrics, and paper towels. Benzene is found in plastics and synthetic fibers. Trichloroethylene is found in inks, paints, varnishes, and adhesives. Ammonia is found in window cleaners and fertilizers. All of these substances are toxic to humans and animals; formaldehyde is a carcinogen.

We don't actually know what effect many indoor chemicals have on our bodies, but there are disturbing suggestions. For example, in the 2010s, thousands of housecats began developing hyperthyroidism, a condition in which the thyroid produces too much of the hormones it secretes to regulate metabolism. The cats lose weight rapidly and will die if untreated. About 10 percent of older cats now have hyperthyroidism—a condition that did not exist in cats before the late 1970s. Researchers have found evidence that the condition might be the result of exposure to polybrominated diphenyl ethers (PBDEs), a type of flame retardant that became common in household goods in the late 20th century. Cats lick themselves daily, so they could easily ingest chemicals that stick to their fur. This is worrisome, because PBDEs are ubiquitous and in nearly everyone's body today.

How can you keep your home from poisoning you? It's not always easy, but there are a few things you can do. Don't buy tons of cleaning products or home scents. Good ventilation goes a long way to keeping air fresh; open windows and use ceiling fans to keep the air moving.

You could also grow plants. Plants naturally suck carbon dioxide out of the air and emit oxygen as a waste product. Plants are so good at cleaning the air that NASA uses them to improve indoor air quality in space. Facilities like space stations must keep their indoor air clean, and they can't just open the window to let in fresh air. NASA's Clean Air study in the 1980s discovered that plants are very good at removing pollutants such as ammonia, benzene, formaldehyde, and trichloroethylene from the air. Good air-cleaning houseplants include Boston fern, spider plant, English ivy, and weeping fig.

## 38. Is there any benefit to using green/natural body care products and cosmetics?

No one wants to wash their hair with a shampoo that releases hazardous chemicals into the air or to brush their teeth with toothpaste that contains carcinogens. Many people buy products labeled "green" or "natural" assuming that these products will not contain any harmful ingredients. Is this actually a good idea?

Harmful ingredients are a real thing. The FDA (U.S. Food and Drug Administration) regulates the ingredients used in personal care products under the Federal Food, Drug, and Cosmetic Act and the Fair Packaging and Labeling Act. For the most part, except for color additives, the FDA does not approve cosmetic products before they go to market. A manufacturer is allowed to sell a product if it is "safe under labeled or customary conditions of use," properly labeled, and not misbranded or adulterated. The safety of cosmetic products is left almost entirely to the companies that make and market the products.

Cosmetic companies do have an interest in customer safety; it does them no good to harm consumers. The industry founded the Cosmetic Ingredient Review (CIR) Expert Panel, which is an independent nonprofit group of scientists who review ingredients and publish their findings. But the level of regulation in the United States is much lower than that in Europe.

The EU bans over 1,000 chemicals from personal care products; the United States has found very few chemicals to be unsafe. The CIR has declared controversial ingredients such as parabens and phthalates to be safe. Toxicity is often dose related—exposure to a small amount of a substance can be harmless. This is why certain potentially dangerous chemicals are allowed. Many consumers disagree.

Phtalates, for example, are endocrine disrupters that have affected the reproductive organs of laboratory animals. Phthalates are common in plastics, soaps, hair sprays, lipstick, and nail polishes. In the early 2000s the Centers for Disease Control and Prevention found that phthalates are present in the bodies of most people. It called for more research, and by 2013 verdict was that phthalates could well be harmful, especially in products for pregnant women and young children. That means that phthalates were allowed to enter people's bodies for 10 years while the research went on; many find that disturbing.

Are natural products the answer? Some consumers believe that anything natural or organic must be better for the skin or body than synthetic substances. This is not necessarily true. Many organic substances are actually bad for skin, and a number of synthetic ingredients are just fine.

The FDA has stated that consumers should not assume that a natural product will be safer or more beneficial than a synthetic one. The USDA organic label is a marketing label, not an indicator of safety. In addition, many products advertised as green or natural are nothing of the kind; these claims are just greenwashing.

It *is* true that many natural ingredients are very good for the skin—olive oil, coconut oil, cocoa butter, shea butter, licorice, and omega three fatty acids are just a few of the naturally occurring ingredients that are excellent for skin and body. But just because something is natural does not mean it is harmless. All fragrances can be potentially irritating. According to cosmetics expert Paula Begoun, anything that makes skin tingle or burn—including alcohol and minty essential oils—can cause the skin to break down.

Even the best natural ingredients will break down if they are exposed to light or air. If you buy natural products, look for opaque packaging that keeps air away from the product, such as a pump. And if you are worried about something, do your research—more and more information becomes available every year.

## 39. What is eco-fashion?

Eco-fashion, or sustainable fashion, is a movement to incorporate sustainability into garment production. Eco-fashion supporters believe that the fashion industry should work to minimize its environmental impact and social destruction.

Current trends in fashion are decidedly not sustainable. Fast fashion is the rule of the day. Clothing production doubled worldwide between 2000 and 2014. Retailers—and customers—want designs to appear in stores as quickly as possible, and to be inexpensive and available in a wide range of sizes. Companies such as Zara manufacture new items constantly and deliver new clothes to stores twice a week. Consumers are barraged with advertising, tempting them to order new clothes for every conceivable occasion. Shoppers scour the Internet for the best bargains, forcing retailers to constantly adjust prices downward.

Producing cheap clothing at that rate has to cost something. The environmental impacts of garment manufacture are enormous. Cotton, for example, makes up half the fibers in garments. Cotton growing destroyed the soil in the South of the United States in just over a century, as topsoil washed away downstream; the cotton economy collapsed during the first half of the 20th century. The soils of the Southeast took thousands of years to form; they will not return anytime soon.

That history has not stopped the world from growing vast amounts of cotton for cheap clothing. Cotton requires lots of water—about 75 percent of cotton grown must be irrigated. Pesticides and herbicides are necessary to keep down bugs and weeds, and the large monoculture fields do not grow well without the addition of industrial fertilizers. All these chemicals can run off into water supplies. Harvesting, cleaning, spinning, and dying cotton fibers use fossil fuels. Scientists estimate that producing 1 kilogram of cotton fabric produces 23 kilograms of greenhouse gases.

If cotton is bad, what fabrics should you wear? Artificial fibers such as polyester, made from fossil fuels, are cheaper to produce than cotton. Some polyester garments can be recycled. But much of the time, polyester fibers are spun with other substances such as cotton to make blends. These blended fabrics really can't be recycled because it takes far too much work to separate out the components.

Rayon is made from plant fibers such as bamboo, which makes it sound environmentally friendly, but the chemicals involved in the process are harmful to workers. Carbon disulfide, for example, can cause heart attacks, strokes, and Parkinson's disease in workers who are exposed to it for years. A market for rayon encourages tropical countries such as Indonesia to plant bamboo—cutting down old-growth forests to create cropland.

Wool comes from sheep, which require space to live and food to eat and emit methane in their digestive gases. Wool, though, requires somewhat less treatment and can last a very long time.

Fabrics are often made in countries with lax environmental regulations. Dyes and other chemicals used in fabric manufacture can contain toxic substances such as lead, arsenic, and mercury. Factory wastewater can be dumped straight into rivers.

The manufacture of clothing is entirely global now. Look at the tags in your clothing; you will see that your wardrobe is extremely cosmopolitan, made in Bangladesh or Nicaragua or Vietnam. Clothing factories are located in places where garments can be produced for the lowest price. This means finding workers who will labor for hours every day for very little pay. As globalization has progressed, the countries that were once reliable factory locations have gotten more economically prosperous and the workers have come to expect higher wages. Manufacturers might then move to a cheaper country.

The garment industry is notorious for exploiting workers, employing young children, or dangerous conditions. The Triangle Shirtwaist Factory fire in 1911 killed 146 young women in New York, leading to improvements in worker safety laws in the United States. Tragedies like that one remain common in places like Bangladesh and India where workers have very few protections.

Finished garments must be shipped to consumers, which can be a very long trip. First the clothes have to come to the United States from their factories. Then they may be trucked around the country to stores or shipped directly to consumers from online retailers. Returns add more carbon emissions to the transport process.

On the consumer side, people buy far more clothes than they can wear. In 2015, people spent $1.8 trillion on clothing. Most people struggle with storing their wardrobes. The Internet is full of guides to organizing closets. Websites describing capsule wardrobes or Marie Kando's method of selecting which items to keep and which to throw away are wildly popular, and still people seem to have more clothes than they know what to do with. Every unworn garment is money wasted, but even so it's easy to see this as just a housekeeping problem.

Or you can just get rid of it. In 2013, almost 13 million tons of textiles went to landfills. Half of the clothing purchased is thrown away within a year; when clothing is so cheap, it's easy to treat it as disposable.

Lots of people donate their unused clothing to charity. This feels good—it's nice to imagine your garments helping a deserving poor person. But what happens to clothes that get donated? Charities such as Goodwill or the Salvation Army carefully sort donations to choose the items they believe will sell. Maybe 10 percent ends up on the sales floor. The rest—and items that remain unsold after several weeks—go to liquidators that purchase clothing by the pound. These clothes may end up in Africa, where they are sold for fractions of their original purchase prices. (African nations are looking at banning these imports, which are harmful to their local garment industries.) The rest of the clothes may be recycled as rags, processed into stuffing for furniture, or sent to landfills.

That is all depressing. What is a green consumer to do?

- Only buy clothes you actually need. Consider using a capsule wardrobe, perhaps customizing it for each season.
- Trade clothes with friends and relatives. It's a fun and free way to get a wardrobe refresh.
- Buy clothing made from organic cotton or wool (organic regulations are quite strict about pesticide and dye use) made with natural dyes.
- Buy high-quality clothing in classic styles that will last for seasons or years instead of falling apart in a couple of months.
- Investigate charities before you donate clothes to them; look for one that has a local market for gently used items.
- Shop at consignment shops or charity stores, which often sell high-quality fashionable items at reasonable prices.
- Mend or alter old garments so you can keep wearing them.

## 40. Is ecotourism actually green?

Ecotourism is environmentally responsible travel. The term generally refers to travel to undisturbed natural areas to appreciate nature and any local human culture that has a low negative impact on the area, promotes conservation, and benefits the local population.

Tourism and mass travel became popular in the 1980s. Before then, most people did not travel far from home or very often. By the 1980s, though, air travel had become inexpensive, and enough people had ready cash to travel for leisure, leading to a proliferation of resorts and tourist facilities.

Conservationists worried about the environmental impact of all this building and activity, which often took place in sensitive landscapes such as wetlands or coral reefs. They proposed a new concept in travel, one that would respect the natural landscape and native human inhabitants of attractive places and that would benefit them rather than damaging them.

Ecotourism emphasizes conservation, biodiversity, and local communities. It often includes an educational component. Proponents believe that it can help communities by bringing in much-needed cash and that the educational aspects make visitors better conservationists. Today ecotourism produces a significant portion of the incomes of nations, including Costa Rica, Madagascar, and Nepal.

Ecotourists might walk instead of using motor vehicles. They may stay in un-air-conditioned shelters built of local materials by local people. They are encouraged to conserve water and electricity. Food is probably local. There may be attention to packaging and food waste.

Sometimes promoting sustainable travel means limiting numbers of visitors. The Galapagos Islands, for example, are very sensitive habitats. The islands impose a strict quota on the number of people who can visit so that tourists do not destroy the unique landscape.

The International Ecotourism Society (TIES) is a nonprofit organization founded in 1990 and dedicated to promoting ecotourism. It has members in over 120 countries. It offers certification in sustainable tourism management, workshops on ecotourism, and a list of ecoDestinations for tourists to choose from. Responsible Travel.com also publishes a list of destinations and guidelines for travelers who want to minimize their environmental impact. Ecotourism vacations include yoga retreats, Italian cooking classes, lemur study in Madagascar, cycling in Cuba, and treks through Mongolia.

Critics of ecotourism claim that there is no such thing as environmentally sound tourism. They use the term "greenwash" to describe activities that advertise themselves as green but are in fact nothing of the kind. Swimming with dolphins may do nothing at all to benefit the local environment, and villagers may give up their farms in order to peddle souvenirs to tourists. They complain that calling travel "ecotourism" lets wealthy Westerners ignore the overall environmental impact of their travel, such as the massive carbon footprint created by long-distance air travel.

Proponents of ecotourism counter that if it were not for tourism, many of the natural areas popular with visitors would have been lost to development by now. The Serengeti remains savanna partly because tourists want to see African wildlife. Rain forests remain intact instead of being cut for timber because local communities are invested in maintaining a landscape that people want to visit.


## 41. I am overwhelmed! How do I set priorities?

If you let yourself think too much about environmental pressures, it's easy to panic. With human populations growing rapidly, governments and corporations operating on a scale you can't even imagine, and drilling into the ocean beds and pumping carbon into the air and pollutants into the water faster than you can blink—what can one individual do to make any difference?

One thing you can do is stop thinking that you yourself can save the world. You can't. You can't save humanity, and you can't stop the extinctions that are already in progress. Take the pressure off yourself.

Then think about what matters most to you. Accepting that environmental destruction is going on around you doesn't mean you have to just give up and live a wasteful, polluting, unconscious life. If green living matters to you, then live green.

This is actually one of the most influential things you can do. The more people become aware of climate change and environmental stewardship, the more fashionable green living becomes, and fashion is a powerful driver of behavior. Remember—back in the 1990s, recycling was a new idea in much of the United States. Today almost everyone at least knows he or she should recycle. Before that, in the 1960s, Americans littered like crazy. An advertising campaign with a weeping Native American coupled with laws fining litterers completely changed that. This has happened with many things—smoking, drunk driving, and lying in the sun to tan (after first getting sunburned) were all considered "normal" before a few people pointed out that they were not great ideas.

So think about your own life. Consider ways you might live green. Then adopt the ones that seem most important or at least easiest to incorporate. Some ideas include the following:

- Buy less. Buy what you need, not just what catches your eye.
- Eat better. Eat whole, natural foods, not processed foods. Eat foods with minimal packaging.
- Consume less. Just in general.
- Look at your home's energy efficiency, and try to improve it.
- Drive less. Bike, carpool, or take public transport if those are possible. If not, at least try to plan your driving for maximum efficiency.
- Do research. Living green means knowing the impact of your actions. That takes work—you have to learn where things come from, how they are made, and where they end up.

Research might lead you to the world of self-reliance. You might want to learn more about raising your own food and other necessities. Our ancestors knew how to provision themselves from the land. Do you know how to grind wheat or how to butcher a chicken? What about spinning wool or cotton into yarn, weaving it into cloth, and making that into clothing? Does it bother you that you don't?

Some people adopt such a green lifestyle that they move themselves completely off the grid. There are different ways to do that. Some go full-on pioneer, living without electricity or running water in log houses and teepees. Others manage to create a modern homestead with wind turbines or solar panels to provide electricity to power pumps so they can have most of the comforts of modernity.

There is a wide range of green activities between a wasteful, unconscious, consumerist lifestyle and living in a cabin in the woods. You can decide how far you want to go with your green living.

## 42. How can I help persuade corporations and businesses to protect the environment?

How can an individual persuade politicians and corporations that protecting the environment is important? Convince them that it will save them money.

Businesses respect the bottom line. They make decisions based on costs and profits; if a practice is not profitable, a corporation will usually not adopt it.

Politicians listen to businesses. They listen to ordinary citizens, too, but part of a politician's job is to facilitate a strong economy. Businesses provide jobs to local citizens and can bring money into communities, so politicians tend to favor them.

Both politicians and businesses may like the idea of protecting the environment, but they do not like to think in terms of fantasy or sentiment. They want numbers. Fortunately, a scientific approach to environmental activism can provide them numbers.

The truth is that during the 20th century most people took natural resources for granted. Air and water went into economic decisions, but often there was no value placed on these resources. Because they were "free," no one thought about the impact on them. Air pollution is a problem largely because of this notion; no one paid attention to what was going into the air from industrial processes or transportation. This phenomenon is known as market failure.

When an actual monetary value is placed on a resource, people are much more likely to use it responsibly. If you have to pay for water, you are careful to use only what you need. If you have to pay for the amount of carbon you put into the air, you will likely try to minimize your costs there.

Scientists and activists who work in the environmental area have learned to identify the value of natural resources. When people can see the actual economic value of a resource, they make very different decisions. So, for example, the value of a mangrove forest might be $1,000 per hectare per year. A number like that could be compared to an alternative use of the land, such as aquaculture development. If the economic benefits of maintaining the mangrove forest outweigh the potential economic development of aquaculture—including all the environmental costs of the aquaculture operation—then it would make sense to politicians to support environmental protection.

At the moment, the pro-business side of things has the advantage of decades of entrenched influence. The study of economics through most of the 20th century didn't take environmental protection into account, either. A new generation of environmental economists is currently correcting this imbalance.

Now you may be thinking, that's all very well, but you're not about to do an economic analysis of every cause. But you still believe that corporations and governments should be forced to care for the environment. What can you do to make a difference?

There are several things that are quick and easy and don't require a major commitment. These include the following:

- Call or write your congressmen. You have representatives at both the state and federal levels. Learn who your federal representatives and senators are. Let them know what you think. It's their job to listen.

- Call or write corporations to complain about their environmental practices. Stop buying products you don't believe in.
- Donate money to causes you believe in.
- Volunteer for causes.
- Blog or post your opinions on social media. Make your opinions known.
- Protests. Marching in the street holding signs is a time-honored way of making your opinion known. Some protests draw massive crowds around the world. The powers that be definitely notice.

And become an informed citizen. The United States already has a large body of environmental law. Read about it, and see how it is being enforced. Follow events around the world. Study science!

Green living is becoming more and more common even as populations and pollution increase. Renewable energy is the energy of the future—it has to be, for practical and economic reasons, though activism certainly plays a role. Things really do change.

# Case Studies

## CASE 1: SHANTI LIVES GREEN FOR A YEAR

Shanti is a 25-year-old college graduate who works full-time. She lives alone. She has been reading about climate change and air pollution and is getting more and more worried. She decides that the best thing she can do for the moment is to think globally but act locally, starting with her own lifestyle. She goes through her life step by step and is daunted by how much she consumes. Can she do anything at all to live green?

Shanti's biggest weakness is shopping for clothing. She loves fashion and she loves shopping, especially Internet shopping, where it is so easy to click a button and order something. Her closet is always stuffed, mostly with things she never wears. She decides that a large wardrobe of disposable, cheap clothing is incompatible with living green.

A capsule wardrobe might be the solution. A capsule wardrobe pares clothing down to the essentials. That means choosing tops, bottoms, dresses, outerwear, and shoes that will fit the season and meet all needs without any excess. Shanti decides to go with a 30-item wardrobe, not counting undergarments and sleepwear. To give herself a little more flexibility, she decides that she will redo her wardrobe every season, so she can adjust it four times a year. Choosing the correct items is surprisingly difficult; she doesn't want to get rid of anything she might need. But she forces herself to go through everything, using Marie Kondo's guide to decluttering, *The Life-Changing Magic of Tidying Up*. She hauls several bags of old clothes to Goodwill. Her closet looks airy and spacious and a little alarming.

Shanti knows that food production is costly to the environment. Meat is especially problematic, but she also worries about contributing to global overfishing. She decides that the most environmentally responsible thing she can do is to adopt a vegetarian diet of primarily local foods. She will make her own lunches to bring to work and eat most other meals at home. She will allow some exceptions for restaurant food—it's hard to make sure that is local, and it would be a shame to completely give up a social life—but she will still stick to her vegetarian diet.

Fortunately for Shanti, she also likes pretty much any vegetable. She starts her plan in the summer. That is easy! The local farmers' markets are full of fresh tomatoes, cucumbers, berries, peaches, and other seasonal delights. The offerings change every month or even every week. She had no idea there were so many kinds of peaches! Local dairy farms produce fresh milk—one even sells raw milk—and she can easily find local cheese and eggs. There is even a local bakery that makes fresh bread.

Shanti's grandmother is an expert food preserver, and she offers to teach Shanti the basics of canning. They buy extra fruits and vegetables from the farmers' market and make jam and pickles. The process is hot and messy, but Shanti loves seeing the jars of strawberry and blackberry and peach jam cooling on the windowsill. She is happy to have that preserved food when winter comes, and a local vegetarian diet is not much fun. The farmers' market is closed and local food is hard to find. It seems that the only local vegetables available are kale and butternut squash. Shanti brings a lentil casserole to Thanksgiving dinner; her brother makes snide comments about hippy activists and doesn't touch it. In December Shanti gives up and buys frozen vegetables from the supermarket just to add some interest back to her diet.

Spring arrives with the new crops of fresh greens and asparagus. Shanti is thrilled to say goodbye to plates of kale and last fall's butternut squash. She looks forward to another year of eating seasonally.

All of Shanti's friends drink water constantly and talk about how important it is to stay hydrated. Many of them buy bottled water in plastic bottles. They recycle these bottles when it's convenient but mostly just toss them in the trash. Some of the water comes from places like Fiji, which seems like a long way to ship a liquid that comes out of the sink. This doesn't seem very green. Shanti buys herself an attractive, lightweight metal bottle and carries it in her backpack. She can refill it anywhere.

Shanti doesn't own a car and would prefer not to buy one. When Shanti starts living green, she is working at a job downtown, just 2 miles from her house. This makes her daily commute easy—she can walk or ride her bike and get exercise in while she travels. Her workplace dress code is casual, and she doesn't mind wearing a raincoat in bad weather.

Shopping is a bit more of a challenge. In the warm months, a farmers' market sets up every weekend near her workplace. It's easy to reach without a car but not so easy to haul home her purchases. Milk is especially heavy! She borrows a friend's bicycle trailer to carry her things, but it's still hard work pedaling it uphill. Most weeks she grabs a ride with someone driving in a car. This feels a little like cheating, but at least they are using the car to transport more than one person.

In the fall, Shanti gets a new job several miles away. It's too far to bike, and she has to dress nicely—incompatible with bicycle commuting, especially on rainy days. Her town has only minimal public transportation. When she looks at the bus schedule, she discovers that she would have to take three different buses to get to work—and that the journey would take over two hours. She reminds herself to petition the local city council for more public transportation and starts looking for a used car with good gas mileage.

But then she considers paying someone else to drive her. Taking a ride service such as Uber to work would cost her $16 every day. This seems like a lot, but when she adds up the cost of car payments, gasoline, parking, and insurance, she discovers that the ride service is actually cheaper. She decides that she doesn't need a car right now. Maybe later on when she has a family she might change her mind, but at the moment a personal vehicle is unnecessary.

Shanti knows that her air conditioner uses a huge amount of power. She decides that, as a committed green person, she should not be responsible for so many carbon emissions. She decides to turn it off. Of course, she could just turn up the thermostat. That would make a difference in emissions and lower her power bills, too. But her grandparents lived in an un-air-conditioned house. At summer camp she has stayed in tents and cabins with no electricity. Her house has ceiling fans. How bad can it be?

May isn't too bad. Nighttime temperatures are lower, so mornings are cool. Shanti tries the Mediterranean method of opening the windows in the morning to let in the cool air and then closing them to keep out the afternoon heat. The curtains can keep out most of the sunlight. With the ceiling fans blowing, it isn't so bad.

When summer arrives in full force, though, things get harder. The house is hot all the time. The curtains make it dark. It's hard to concentrate on working. She finds herself napping during the hottest part of the day—the heat is easiest to tolerate if she doesn't move too much. The nights are hot. The sheets get sweaty. It's hard to sleep. The fans make noise, which is irritating. None of her friends will visit.

To cope, Shanti dresses in light, flowing layers, which help air circulate. She discovers the pleasure of sitting on the shady porch with an icy glass of lemonade. Taking showers provides temporary relief. She goes to the pool every day if she can find the time. Visiting places with air conditioning—a grocery store, the mall, the movies—is a delightful treat.

By August, though, Shanti is about to lose her mind. She has an important project to complete, and she can't think if she is stuck to her chair with sweat. She closes the windows, turns on the air conditioner, and breathes a sigh of relief. That night she gets a good night's sleep for the first time in months. She feels a little bit like a failure, but she doesn't care because it feels so good to be cool.

Having spent the summer enduring the heat without an air conditioner, Shanti decides to see if she can manage without her heater. Winters in her area aren't terribly cold; temperatures go below freezing only a few times. When temperatures drop in October, Shanti starts wearing sweaters in the house. It's not too bad until around Thanksgiving, when the nights have been cold for a while and the house itself seems colder.

Living in a cold house at first seems easier than living in a hot one. Shanti can always wear more clothes. She gets thin insulating long underwear and wears it under her clothes. She finds that wool, cashmere, and fleece are all good for keeping warm. A lightweight down jacket and wool cap become part of her inside uniform in the coldest months. She makes the bed to keep her warm. She is astonished at how expensive a thick down comforter is but decides it is a sensible investment because it will provide years of nighttime warmth and allow her to keep her bedroom cold at night.

Her hands and feet give her the most trouble. She can't type with gloves on, and while fingerless gloves help some, they leave her fingertips freezing. Her feet are especially hard to keep warm. Slippers feel useless when her feet have turned to blocks of ice. She finally arrives at a combination of warm socks, fleece-lined boots, and legwarmers that can keep the blood in her toes. At night she sleeps with socks and down booties on her feet. She buys an electric blanket because even with the down comforter she is still cold.

Finally, the real freezes arrive. Shanti's feet and hands are so cold at her desk that she can't work at all. Her tiny space heater just isn't enough. Just before Christmas, she caves in and turns on the central heating. She keeps it on until the weather warms up.

## Analysis

Consumerism is a huge problem for the environment. Huge amounts of resources are wasted on disposable clothing and other items. Shanti's experience with reducing her wardrobe, which is just a drop in the bucket, at least allows her to see what she really uses. Once Shanti has narrowed her wardrobe down to the essentials, she finds it refreshingly easy to get dressed. Because she doesn't allow herself to buy anything on impulse, she loses interest in online shopping, which makes it easier to concentrate on work. When her credit card statements arrive, they are surprisingly low—she hadn't realized how much money she was spending on clothes until she stopped buying them. And once in a while, she does succumb to temptation. She needs a dress for a wedding and finds the perfect designer dress on sale. She buys it, and it feels especially gratifying because it's a special treat.

Shanti's friends tell her that she needs to eat meat and that she will become unhealthy if she eats only vegetables. This is not true at all; much of the world's population never eats meat. Shanti's own 86-year-old grandmother is a complete vegan, has never eaten an animal product, and is perfectly healthy. Shanti considers veganism but decides that she likes eggs and dairy products too much; she can't imagine giving up ice cream!

Eating an entirely local diet can be difficult, especially if you live in an area where winters shut down agricultural production entirely. Frozen vegetables are not a bad choice. They aren't local, but at least they are not as polluting as meat, and in many cases frozen veggies are both healthy and not as carbon intensive as fresh ones.

A reusable water bottle is a great idea, and it makes use of a ubiquitous, high-quality resource: tap water. The tap water in Shanti's town is excellent. It costs next to nothing. It has fluoride in it, which is good for teeth.

Because green living involves knowing why you are doing things, Shanti also does a little research on human water requirements. She discovers that people don't actually need to drink eight glasses of water a day. This is a myth. There is no scientific evidence that anything bad happens to a person who doesn't drink constantly. It seems that this myth came from a report in 1945 that found that people need to consume about 2.5 liters of water a day—most of which they get from the food they eat. Doctors report that they almost never see cases of dehydration—it's just not a real concern.

Transportation is one of the biggest difficulties for green living. In many parts of the United States, a car is a necessity. Jobs, schools, stores, and homes are too far apart to walk, and public transportation is inadequate to nonexistent. Roads are too dangerous to bicycle, even when distances are not too great. But there is some hope for the future. Alternative fuel vehicles, ride-sharing, and telecommuting all offer possible ways to reduce carbon footprints associated with transport.

Through her air conditioning experiment, Shanti has gained a real appreciation of the wonders of modern climate control and will no longer take it for granted. She saved several hundred dollars on her power bill. And she now knows that it is entirely possible for her to live without air conditioning if she has to. A century ago everyone did, and much of the world still does today.

Heating is another concern. In many parts of the world, people could freeze to death in their own homes if they didn't heat them. Central heating is a luxury that is still not available in many places. Shanti's strategies of wearing more clothes inside and using thick bedding are time-honored ways of surviving cold temperatures, so is heating small areas and modifying how space is used. The Japanese kotatsu, for example, heats just the area under a table, holding the heat in with a quilt. Everyone sits around the kotatsu with their legs under the quilt, using the small table as an eating and working surface. It works well in houses with no central heating at all.

After a year, Shanti takes stock. Living green was both easier and harder than she thought it would be. She has made some permanent changes in her life—using ceiling fans and windows for natural ventilation, dressing for the weather before using climate control, thinking about her food. In the coming years, she will remember the lessons from this year and use them to make decisions about how to live. She may not always choose the greenest option, but at least she will think before she acts.

## CASE 2: JAMAL WANTS TO REDUCE FOOD WASTE

Jamal is a senior at a large public high school. He is seriously concerned about the amount of waste his high school produces. Every single day the trash barrels overflow with food, paper napkins, plastic cutlery, plastic wrappers, all jumbled together. Much of the food goes straight from lunch line to tray to garbage. And yet his friends complain about being hungry. This makes no sense at all. Jamal decides to look into the issue to see what might be done. He discovers that it is extremely complicated.

Obviously part of the problem is that the students just aren't eating the food they are given. Jamal wonders if there is some way to get them to eat more. One problem is that students simply don't like the food on offer. Jamal is surprised to learn how many ideas he finds to make food more appetizing. Simply giving foods attractive names is surprisingly effective. Adding smoothie stations is a popular technique; students are happy to drink fruits and vegetables.

Jamal's school cafeteria just has big trash bins, and students throw everything in them. Some days nearly half of the food thrown away is untouched. There is a large needy community nearby that could be eating this food. But no one is allowed to take uneaten food off campus, and the school administrators are convinced that donating food to charities is difficult.

Jamal investigates food donation and discovers that it actually could be done. Donating leftover school lunch food to food banks is legal and encouraged by the U.S. Department of Agriculture (USDA). Schools can work with charities to organize pickups. Some states provide guidelines to help schools donate their food. A school might be able to work with nonprofit organizations such as Food Bus (www.foodbus.org), a public charity that organizes donation of uneaten food from elementary schools. Jamal decides it would be best to approach a PTA representative about the initial organization. Once the program is designed, student groups could handle the daily work.

Jamal signs his school up as a participant with the School Cafeteria Discards Assessment Project, run by the Environmental Research and Education Foundation (EREF). The EREF is a nonprofit charitable research organization that funds scientific research and educational initiatives into waste management practices. It is working to quantify the amount of food and other materials wasted by schools. The simplest level of participation consists of filling out a single questionnaire, but Jamal signs on for the highest level of commitment, agreeing to weigh the waste in cafeteria bins 6–10 times over a 90-day period. The school already has an appropriate shipping scale in the science laboratory.

Half-eaten food can't be donated. It can, however, be composted. The city of San Francisco, for example, now requires that all food waste be composted, including food waste at schools. Jamal realizes that this is an opportunity for the science teachers to get involved in a real-world project. A compost program is a great way to teach students about ecological cycles and the difference between various types of waste products. There are many ways to compost. Jamal explores the different scientific experiments that the students could do. They can examine the temperature of the pile and see how it climbs and then drops as microorganisms consume the available nutrients. They can see how effective it is as a fertilizer. They can even buy worms to accelerate the composting process. The Cornell Waste Management Institute in the Department of Crop and Soil

Sciences has good information on composting on its website (compost .css.cornell.edu/).

If lunch waste is going to turn into compost, the school could plant a garden to make use of it. Jamal wants to get a garden started but doesn't know anything about gardening. He knows someone who does, though—his biology teacher. She has already taught the class lessons on ecology, plant science, and soils. She agrees to help plant the garden if Jamal will find funding for it. He also has to talk to the lunchroom manager to see if the lunchroom can use vegetables from the garden.

By the end of the school year, Jamal, his classmates, and the other people who work with the school have made some real changes. It may take years for the school's food and garbage problems to disappear, but he at least sees that there is the potential for change.

### Analysis

School lunchrooms waste tons of food. Literally—in England, schools throw away about 123,000 tons of food every year, accounting for 13 percent of nondomestic food waste. In Los Angeles, students throw away at least $100,000 worth of food every day, which amounts to $18 million a year. A 2013 study found that students at two Boston middle schools did not eat nearly all the food they were served, discarding over $430,000 worth of edible food. The researchers extrapolated that nationally, some $1.2 billion is wasted on school lunches every year. Most of this food goes straight to landfills, where it really does go to waste.

School waste echoes overall national trends. In the United States, between 30 and 40 percent of the food supply is wasted. This food could go to help families in need, but for various reasons it can't reach them. Most of this food goes to landfills, where if it decomposes it can release the greenhouse gas methane. All the resources that go into producing the food—land, water, fossil fuels, labor, transportation, preparation, storage—are lost.

This is a well-known problem, and people are trying to solve it. In 2015 the USDA announced the first national food loss and waste goal, a reduction of 50 percent by 2030. The USDA's Food Waste Challenge calls on all food providers—farmers, processors, grocery stores, schools, restaurants, local governments that handle waste management—to reduce waste, recover what food they can for charities, and recycle and compost everything else. Jamal's school could participate in this effort. If it reduces its waste 50 percent by 2030, it could become a U.S. Food Loss and Waste 2030 Champion.

Only 2 percent of U.S. children eat the recommended number of fruits and vegetables. The effects of a poor diet are obvious—obesity has skyrocketed in recent years, along with diabetes and other conditions that accompany high body fat. Simultaneously, many Americans are malnourished, failing to consume the necessary nutrients for good health. The reasons for this phenomenon are perhaps beyond the ability of schools to solve, but nevertheless schools are required to try.

In the United States, school lunches are governed by federal laws administered by the USDA. The Health, Hunger-Free Kids Act of 2010 attempted to reform school lunch programs to make them healthier. It sets standards for all food sold at schools during the school day, including food sold in cafeterias, from school stores, from vending machines, and at fund-raisers.

One requirement is that school districts now offer fresh produce, both fruits and vegetables, and that every student take at least one. If a school does not, it can't receive federal reimbursement for meals. Food experts say that this is necessary because the best way to persuade anyone to eat a food is regular exposure to it; making kids put vegetables on their plates might eventually result in them eating those vegetables.

Some school lunch providers disagree, observing that this is a perfect recipe for food waste. They think it would make more sense to stop forcing kids to take foods they don't want. A survey in 2013 found that the fresh fruit/vegetable requirement cost school districts nationwide $5.4 million every day, $3.8 million of which was being thrown straight in the trash. Students apparently don't want to eat the fresh produce.

Kids eat more when they like their food. School lunches are notoriously awful; attempts to make them healthier don't always make them taste better.

Schools have experimented with improving the quality of lunches. Celebrity chefs have developed menus. Having real cooks prepare real food has reduced waste dramatically in some schools. In the United Kingdom, school managers have found that improving menus really does help, as does monitoring what the students eat. On the other hand, this doesn't always work—waste can continue despite gourmet menus—and this strategy is difficult or impossible for many schools in the United States because they no longer have actual kitchens with real cooking facilities.

The Smarter Lunchrooms Movement (www.smarterlunchrooms.org) has numerous strategies for improving lunch. For example, attractive presentation can work wonders. Students prefer to eat fruits and vegetables that are already cut up—they actually eat two-thirds more when the fruit is cut, and they are much more likely to eat raw veggies that come with a dip. Placing fruit and vegetable in multiple locations in the service line, one of which is right next to the cash register, increases the odds that it will be eaten. Naming a fruit of the day and giving it a colorful display is also helpful. Apparently most students do take and eat at least some of the daily entrée, so cafeterias can put veggies in those—think tacos with lettuce and tomato, or beef and broccoli stir-fry. Schools can offer special taste tests throughout the year, where students are encouraged to try something they've never had before or are convinced they don't like.

Schools in Utah have experimented with rewarding students who eat more produce. They give them raffle tickets or even small cash prizes if they eat their vegetables.

Some flexibility can reduce waste. Simply allowing different portion sizes makes good sense; students with small appetites will naturally eat less than large football players. Share tables are tables where students are allowed to swap food with one another. This can include school lunch items as well as food they have brought from home. These tables are legal, and the USDA encourages them.

Then there is timing. Younger kids eat more when they have recess before lunch. Recess gives them time to burn off excess energy and build up an appetite so they don't feel restless while they are sitting down to eat. A break for older students could work as well.

Giving students more time to eat usually helps them eat more. Schools with 30-minute lunch periods, which is supposed to result in 25 minutes of time seated at a table (your mileage may vary depending on how rapidly your lunch line moves and how lucky you are), have less food waste than schools with shorter lunch periods.

Student engagement with food can work wonders. One reason students throw away so much food is that they have no relationship at all to it; they don't know where it comes from, they don't choose it, and disposing of it is not their problem. Students who are given choice and responsibility for their school environment often rise to the occasion.

This isn't an outrageous idea. In Japan, high school students take care of the school building. They clean the classrooms and offices every day, organizing themselves into teams to cover every job. It doesn't take very long, and it gives the students a sense of possession—they aren't likely to trash a room that they will have to clean up themselves.

Lunch waste programs are a great way for students to get involved. A school might have an eco-team of students who are responsible for ensuring that waste is put into the correct bins—they watch to make sure that food goes into the compost, recyclable materials go in the recycling bins, and uneaten food is collected and held in separate refrigerators for donation.

A UK elementary school has gotten around the wasted fruit problem by implementing "fruity Fridays," in which students chop up the week's leftover fruit to make fruit cocktail. Another school had the students do a project on food waste, in which they donned rubber gloves and sorted through garbage bins to see what was in them; the students then sorted it into materials that could be recycled or composted.

Donated food is really needed; milk and other food are expensive, and many food pantries do not have any reliable source of milk. Programs like this depend on volunteers to transport the food from schools to food banks; these volunteers can be from the PTA or the community, or they can be students themselves.

Setting up a food donation program can take six to eight months—most of a school year. Someone will have to investigate county and state regulations on food donations, find and persuade a local food pantry to take the school's donations, set up a system of volunteers, and arrange for necessary equipment. The school may not have storage for food that will be donated; someone may need to acquire a separate refrigerator to store donations during the week.

In his research Jamal finds some amazing garden success stories. For example, a middle school in Florida grows plants and fish together in an aquaponics system. They grow 15–16 acres worth of food in an indoor space of about 1,800 square feet. The plants grow in stacked towers, and water pumps are powered by a solar battery—a system invented by the students. The kids raise catfish and tilapia, which they can release into the wild or sell to a local fish market. The students make all decisions, from design choices to troubleshooting to what to do with their harvests. They have researched treatments for strawberry fungus, bought ladybugs to eat parasitic insect pests, and created their own systems for germinating tomato seeds.

Other schools have done equally incredible things. A high school in Austin, Texas, has built a garden as a teaching tool for the school's culinary program. The vegetables and fruit are self-sustaining, and the school harvests rainwater for irrigation. A high school in the Bronx is experimenting with urban gardening with a hydroponic rooftop garden. Some schools even raise bees and sell the honey.

There are numerous organizations that provide grants to schools that want to create gardens. The more students engage with the natural world, the better they understand how it works and how important ecological processes are to human existence, so school gardens are popular.

## CASE 3: ROSIE HELPS HER PARENTS BUILD A GREEN HOME

Rosie is a 20-year-old student at a community college. She hopes to work for a green architectural firm after she graduates. As it happens, Rosie's parents are building a new house. She decides to help them make it as green as possible.

First Rosie considers the greenest possibility of all—living entirely off the grid. Plenty of people manage to do this. A couple in Ireland, for example, live in a house made of salvaged timber, stones, and hay bales coated with plaster—the hay insulates the walls. The floor is insulated with a layer of wine bottles. They generate their own electrical power with solar panels and a wind turbine. Their refrigerator is a bucket kept underground; it works well for milk. Though they are not totally self-sufficient for food, they grow all their own vegetables and fruits. They treat their sewage in a septic tank and send the products to a nearby field. All their furniture is made of salvaged materials.

When she proposes this plan to her parents, though, they are not at all keen on it. She agrees that she isn't ready to embrace the 19th-century pioneer lifestyle either, so she looks into green building techniques that are more compatible with modern life.

There are some carbon-neutral homes being built, especially in Europe, but that technology is not yet readily available in the United States. Rosie and her parents decide that a LEED-certified builder can help them create the house they want. In the United States, the LEED (Leadership in Energy and Environmental Design) program, developed by the U.S. Green Building Council, certifies buildings that meet certain standards of energy efficiency. It provides standards for homes and other buildings. The U.S. Green Building Council is a nonprofit group of designers, engineers, architects, builders, and others who are dedicated to sustainable construction. LEED-certified houses are not up to the Passive House standard, but they are much more energy efficient than conventional construction. LEED buildings also typically have better indoor air quality.

According to Energy.gov, energy efficiency is the most cost-effective way to reduce energy used on heating and cooling. Rosie considers two main possibilities for climate control: a geothermal heat pump and a passive solar system. Rosie and her parents decide that the passive solar system will work the best with their lot and design wishes. Good air circulation can improve the performance of any climate control system by moving air around. Rosie decides to install ceiling fans in all the rooms that can hold them. That way her family can set the thermostats a little lower in winter and higher in summer without noticing a difference in comfort.

For a passive solar system to work well, most of the windows have to face south. (This applies to houses in the Northern Hemisphere; in the Southern Hemisphere, the sun's rays would come from the north instead.) The east, west, and north sides of the house will have only as many windows as they need to let in light. Rosie's search turns up a range of energy-efficient windows that have met the Energy Star performance criteria. To add extra light to the house and eliminate the need to use artificial light in the daytime, Rosie adds some skylights to the design.

Because the house's main façade will face south, Rosie decides that they can install solar panels. Her state offers a rebate for part of the cost of installation. The panels should last about 20–30 years, and Rosie has read that solar panels add thousands of dollars to a house's resale value. In addition to the solar panels on the roof, the system will need a controller between the solar panels and the batteries, batteries to store electricity, and an inverter to convert energy from the batteries into household electrical current.

Since the house is already maximizing solar energy, Rosie wants to install a solar water heater. To persuade her parents to go along with the plan, she chooses an active solar water heating system, which will maintain their supply of hot water even in the winter. As a backup, they can install an on-demand water heater for the bathrooms, so that no one needs to take cold showers if the sun hasn't shone for days in the winter.

To further minimize household energy use, Rosie researches appliances to find the most energy-efficient ones, all Energy Star certified. Her mother insists on a clothes drier but agrees to install a drying rack in the south-facing yard so that they can air-dry laundry when the weather is good.

Their LEED builder recommends that the house be built of structural insulated panels (SIPs). SIPs are panels made of a foam core sandwiched between two exterior faces of a material called oriented strand board. They are made in factories to specific dimensions. Because they do not need to be cut to size at the construction site, they can make assembling a building very quick. A shorter building time with less waste can offset the higher cost of the materials.

Rosie wants to grow a vegetable garden so that she can provide at least some of her family's food. The south-facing side of the house has a large sunny space—part of the passive solar design plan—which will give her plenty of room for this garden. For the landscaping around the house itself, she wants to use native plants. Natives provide habitat and resources for native insects and are already adapted to living in the local climate. This will allow them to thrive through weather that would kill typical ornamental plants from the garden center, most of which come from plants native to distant lands such as Asia and that have since been intensively bred for looks, not hardiness. Natives shouldn't need excessive water, fertilizers, or pesticides. She consults her local native plant society's website for some suggestions.

The vegetable garden, however, has to have water. For that, she decides to take advantage of the large square footage of the roof by installing rain barrels. Every inch of rain that falls on 1,000 square feet can produce 600 gallons of rainwater—which means that enough rain falls on the roof to easily water a garden. Of course, she has no intention of catching and storing all this rainwater. Instead, she will set up rain barrels under the downspouts of the gutters. Water will pour straight into these barrels, and she can use that to water the vegetables.

A garden is the perfect way to use up her household organic waste. Rosie's family can save scraps from preparing fruits and vegetables along with wasted food and put all of it in a compost bin where it will turn into free fertilizer and soil amendments. She decides to get two compost bins and place them side by side so that when one gets full it can sit and compost while the other one fills up. She puts them close enough to the rain barrels so that she can use them as a source of water to keep the compost moist.

When it is completed, the house is pleasant, attractive, and comfortable. When done well, green building done with modern materials and techniques allows for the construction of houses that offer all the modern amenities with considerably reduced carbon emissions and energy costs.

### Analysis

Green building is environmentally responsible, sustainable building. It uses resources efficiently. It reduces pollution and waste. It provides good indoor air quality by using nontoxic building materials. Those materials should also be ethically produced. The design should adapt to a changing environment.

Green building has been popular in Europe for some years, and now entire neighborhoods and cities in Europe are becoming carbon neutral. Carbon-neutral homes do not add to the net carbon in the atmosphere. Carbon neutrality can be accomplished by absorbing carbon to make up for carbon emissions—this is how carbon offsets work—but green homes try not to produce emissions at all.

In Malmö, Sweden, a district called Västra Hamnen is completely carbon neutral. Built entirely after 2000, it uses no air conditioners or external heaters. An underground storage system takes natural hot water from underground, uses wind energy to pump it up to heat houses in winter, and then reuses the cooled water to cool buildings in summer. Homes built in areas with geothermal resources (hot groundwater) have a big advantage when it comes to underground heating systems.

In 2015, scientists in the United Kingdom designed a zero-carbon house that sends more power to the grid than it uses. The house has solar panels installed in the south-facing roof. These panels allow light through and they are installed in the roof, not on it, so they function as skylights, allowing the house to be naturally lit in the daytime. A battery can store energy generated by the solar panels. This runs the electrical power system, which powers a heat pump, LED (light-emitting diode) lighting, and home appliances, as well as the ventilation and hot water systems. Heating air is warmed by the solar system and a warm water tank. The walls are heavily insulated to keep the interior temperature consistent.

In 2008 a house built in McLean, Virginia, was hailed as the first carbon-neutral house on the east coast of the United States. It used a geothermal heating and cooling system, a solar hot water heater, solar panels and wind turbines to generate electricity, low-energy LED lighting, rain-capture devices and low-flow water appliances, insulated panels, and a green roof.

Germany's Passive House Institute has been pioneering the design of homes that are extremely energy efficient. Passive houses use the sun, internal heat sources, and heat recovery for heating and passive cooling techniques such as shading. An airtight seal keeps indoor temperatures consistent. The roof and walls are highly insulated, and the windows are specially designed to keep heat in or cold out. A ventilation system brings in fresh air.

People who live in passive houses have very minimal heating and cooling bills, perhaps 10 percent those of a normal house. The building techniques work in all climates, hot and cold. As of 2017, there were very few Passive House–certified homes in the United States, and almost no builders knew much about them, but interest was starting to appear in certain areas.

A geothermal heat pump uses the constant temperature of the ground to heat and cool a building. Unlike air temperatures, ground temperatures are pretty consistent year-round, ranging from 45°F to 75°F. This is typically warmer than a winter air temperature and cooler than summer air temperature. A ground heat exchanger uses this constant temperature to warm or cool a liquid that then circulates through the building. A horizontal heat pump system buries pipes in trenches 5 or 6 feet deep next to the house. Because this house is new construction and there is ample space, this system should fit.

A passive solar design uses energy efficiency to reduce the need for heating and cooling and solar energy to supply those needs. The house collects heat when the sun shines through its windows and then traps that heat in flooring materials—tile, brick, or stone—called thermal mass. The flooring stores the heat during the day and then releases it at night. For this to work, the windows have to face south. Fortunately, the lot has plenty of open space on the south end with no other buildings or large trees, so the house can be situated with a good exposure to southern sun. In order to keep the house from getting too hot in the summer, they add a retractable awning and shutters to block the summer sun.

Windows are one of the biggest sources of energy loss in normal houses. The sun shining on a window can heat the air inside the house—not desirable in the summer. Windows leak, letting in winter cold air. Her parents' old house has old storm windows that never did much to keep out the cold. They hung heavy curtains, which helped some but kept the house dark.

All windows are rated by performance criteria such as air leakage and solar heat gain coefficient (SHGC), which is how much solar energy gets through. For passive solar heating, the south-facing windows should have a high SHGC, to let in lots of heat in the winter. The other windows in the house need a low SHGC so that they reflect heat away. A low-e coating is a microscopic layer of metal oxides that makes them reflective.

SIPs are popular in green building because they can produce a highly airtight house. An ordinary home loses about 40 percent of its heating and cooling to air leakage. SIP homes are 15 times more airtight. SIPs contain wood, but they use it efficiently because they are made from small wood chips instead of entire boards; they are also made from fast-growing tree species in managed forests. SIP homes are typically made airtight, which means the windows do not open. This actually allows for better control over ventilation and humidity levels, which reduce mold problems. The adhesives used in SIPs do not contain volatile organic compounds or formaldehyde.

Sustainably built homes still tend to be slightly more expensive to build than conventional homes, but the difference is not huge. After this initial cost, green houses typically cost much less to operate—some buildings end up requiring no outside electricity at all. Green buildings provide environmental, economic, and social benefits. On the social side, they are healthier for people. They have less polluted indoor air, better ventilation, and better light. This helps people think and sleep better. Green buildings save money on utilities and tend to sell for better prices. They consume less water and electricity and produce fewer emissions.

## CASE 4: JASON WANTS TO TAKE A GREEN VACATION

Jason is a 19-year-old sophomore at a state university, majoring in sustainability studies. He is planning his spring break trip and wants to cause as little environmental damage as possible.

Some of Jason's friends are going on a camping trip. This is going to be real backpacking—they are hiking, carrying everything in their backpacks. They will stay in tents every night. They've mapped a route through the local mountains that will take them through some interesting natural terrain. Because they have chosen an end-to-end hike, they have two choices for transportation. They can drive two vehicles, leaving one at the end point and one at the starting point; the beginning and end of the hike will be enlivened by dropping off and picking up the extra cars. Or they can pay a local shuttle service that offers to take them to the trailhead so they can just leave one car at their destination. This is a little expensive but saves them tons of driving and so should reduce emissions at least a little. The carbon emissions of the shuttle service are somewhat mitigated by the fact that several people can share the ride.

Jason isn't sure he wants to be that green. He considers a staycation—just staying put and enjoying spring break where he lives. But what can he do for entertainment? There are always videos and computer games—Jason actually thinks a week of binge-watching and sleeping late has some appeal. He wonders if there are enough outside activities to keep him occupied for a week. The city where he lives has several museums and parks. There is a theme park an hour's drive away; roller coasters and junk food aren't especially green, but he wouldn't have to go very far. He and his friends could organize cookouts. It might not be a terrible way to decompress in the midst of a hard semester.

Jason has a bicycle that he uses to get around campus. He likes riding it. Maybe a spring break bike trip would be fun! But would it be green? Unless he rides his bike right off campus, Jason will have to travel to cycle. That would involve driving or flying, and possibly transporting his bike (it is possible to rent bikes in most places), but the cycling itself wouldn't produce any emissions. And there are lots of possibilities for adventure. Yellowstone National Park, for example, opens its roads to cyclists in March and April, right at college spring break time. The roads are freshly plowed, and the tourists are not yet invited in. That could be exciting.

Jason and his friends could drive to Florida for some sun, sand, and surf. Jason has read that driving is greener than flying. He and his buddies could cram into a hotel or a condominium. If they spent all their days out on the sand and in the water, they wouldn't consume much, and they could work on their tans.

Jason wonders if he could have a real vacation and still be green. Could he, for example, fly to Mexico? It wouldn't have to be to a spring break party resort in Cancun; he could go to an eco-resort, or even to a place where he could volunteer. Jason has read that it is actually first-class passengers and private jets that produce the vast majority of per capita emissions and that flying coach is barely more polluting than driving, but his friends are not convinced. So many of his friends consider flying the biggest of all carbon offenses that Jason has considered giving up flying entirely.

Jason likes the idea of doing something good for the planet or humanity. He wonders if he should spend his spring break volunteering. Volunteering on vacation, sometimes called voluntourism, has become very popular. Back in 2008, already some 1.6 million people were volunteering on vacation, and numbers have only climbed since then. Volunteers may build schools or houses, teach English, or care for orphans. They get to have a vacation in an interesting place and also feel as if they are doing good. Jason doesn't really want to take on all the logistics himself, so he starts investigating organized voluntourism possibilities, starting with his own college.

Jason has always wanted to travel abroad. Jason is tempted by the Galapagos Islands Volunteer Vacation. The group would climb the cliffs, snorkel the coral reefs, and work on sea turtle and giant tortoise conservation projects in one of the most unique habitats in the world. The price? Over $4,000. Closer to home, the Virgin Islands Volunteer Vacation and Yosemite Volunteer Vacations are more reasonably priced but would still be expensive ways to work through spring break—and Jason would still have to fly. He isn't sure the money or the carbon cost would be worthwhile.

### Analysis

A backpacking camping trip is a very green choice. While Jason's friends are camping, they make a point of keeping their campsites pristine. They pack out all their own trash and even collect garbage they find along the trail. They bring along a stove to cook because building campfires can be environmentally destructive. They purify water from streams. For bathing, they have biodegradable soap that won't harm natural water supplies.

Because they are not using electricity, transportation, or municipal water for several days, their carbon footprint is close to nil. This seems like the greenest option of them all, though at the cost of considerable sacrifices—clean clothes, comfortable beds, toilets, shelter from rain, computers, and phones.

The staycation could be another very green option. One of the greenest things Jason could do is to simply stay put. That doesn't mean being bored. Staycations—vacations in which you stay home—are popular, especially with people on limited budgets and stress-filled daily lives. Staycations give people the chance to relax at home and explore local offerings that they may never otherwise take advantage of.

How green a bike trip is depends on the details. Carrying a tent and camping gear is, of course, very green. It can make a trip more strenuous, though; panniers full of gear are heavy, and you really notice the weight pedaling uphill. Some cyclists prefer "credit card camping," in which they carry just extra clothing and toiletries and spend their nights in hotels or motels along the route. Tour companies organize cycling trips at various levels of luxury; price is the issue there. Many colleges also offer spring break trips organized by students; joining a group of like-minded students could make for a satisfying and environment-friendly vacation.

For the beach trip, driving would probably be greener than flying. Flying is actually less carbon intensive than it used to be, largely because planes are crammed so full of passengers. But if at least two people ride in the car, driving will probably produce fewer emissions per person. They can limit emissions further by always observing the posted speed limit. Driving would also be much cheaper for Jason and his friends to drive, and the car would be useful. They could use it to buy groceries, for example, so that they would not have to eat in restaurants for every meal. If they rent a condominium, they will be able to really control the environmental impact of their food by cooking for themselves. If they spend all their time playing in the waves and avoid fossil-fuel-intensive activities such as riding waverunners or motorboats, they won't emit too much carbon. They should avoid working on their tans, though; ultraviolet radiation is actually a carcinogen and causes skin cancer.

Jason and his friends could stay in a hotel, but that would not be the greenest choice. Hotels are one of the more wasteful aspects of the travel industry. Collectively, hotels consume tremendous amounts of water, electricity, and other resources. A guest staying in a hotel generally uses more resources than he or she would at home; in some places, hotel guests consume twice the water of local residents. Hotel guests have zero incentive to conserve water, so they shower and flush with abandon. Housekeeping might change sheets and towels daily, creating massive piles of laundry. Air conditioning or heat runs constantly, generating emissions. Hotels also generate more waste. Tourist infrastructure has caused severe environmental degradation in many parts of the world.

Airplanes emit huge amounts of carbon. It is an article of faith among many eco-conscious people that if you fly, you are contributing more than your share of carbon to the atmosphere. (Jason does wonder—if he doesn't fly, those flights will take off anyway, so maybe it makes no difference whether he is on them or not. Surely the amount he flies isn't enough to persuade airlines to stay in business and maintain all their routes.)

To mitigate the damage of flying, Jason looks into carbon offsets. Offsets have been popular with large companies for several years because they give them a way to make up for the pollution they emit in their daily business. Airlines today offer passengers the option to purchase carbon offsets along with their tickets. The airlines work with organizations such as the Nature Conservancy to create carbon sinks around the world. Delta Airlines, for example, has used carbon offset payments to purchase forests in Chile to prevent them from being developed, which was calculated to prevent nearly half a million ton of carbon dioxide from being emitted. For an extra few dollars, Jason can rest assured that he has done something to offset the carbon emitted from a flight.

Of course, there is considerable criticism of carbon offset programs. There is the possibility that consumers will stop worrying about emissions if they believe they can mitigate them by simply spending a few dollars more for their airplane tickets. Companies that buy carbon offsets may accelerate their own pollution. Consumers don't always know for sure that their offset payments are actually going to a real project. There is also the problem of how those carbon offsets are executed. Forest projects in the third world affect the local people who live in those areas, and carbon offsets have been implicated in evicting residents from their homes.

On the other hand, critics point out that volunteers may not be doing much good and may actually be harming the recipients of their charity. Volunteer builders are not always very skilled at the work, and they replace local workers who might be paid for the job. There have been reports of fake orphanages set up to attract volunteers who pay money for the privilege of caring for children. The money that volunteers spend on their own travel might be better used as donations that the local community could put to work.

The logistics of volunteer or adventure tours get a little complicated. To make the whole process easier, there are tour operators who can provide a full ecotour or voluntourism adventure. Some colleges organize spring break adventure/volunteer trips. Maryville College in Maryville, Tennessee, for example, has organized both low-impact, long-distance cycling trips and volunteer vacations that help local communities. In the fall of 2016, forest fires ravaged the mountains near the school; that year's Alternative Spring Break went to work on the cleanup.

The American Hiking Society runs Volunteer Vacations that build and maintain hiking trails. Its Alternative Break is a program specifically for college students on spring break. It organizes volunteer crews of 6–15 people who backpack or day hike and spend their days engaged in hard physical labor. Volunteers spend their nights in cabins, bunkhouses, or tents at primitive campsites. Food is provided. Groups can go together, or individual students can join. Registration costs are quite reasonable ($195 for students in 2017), although participants have to pay their own travel costs to get to the job site.

The United Way runs a program called Alternative Spring Break. Through its student branch, Student United Way, it organizes week-long service projects throughout the United States. Projects include building, youth education activities, and garden cultivation. Trips are open to anyone 18 and older, alone or in a group. The trips are inexpensive, about $300–400 in 2017, and include meals, housing, and local transportation.

Projects Abroad (www.projects-abroad.org) offers a variety of spring break trips aimed at both college and high school students. These trips go to countries outside the United States; the majority go to nearby countries to cut down on travel time and jet lag, though some trips go to Africa or Fiji in the South Pacific. Trips include building houses and toilet facilities in Jamaica, caring for children in Belize or Costa Rica, nature conservation in Mexico, or shadowing doctors in Argentina. These trips are quite expensive, though.

The REI Adventures program (www.rei.com/adventure) offers a range of trips in a wide variety of locations. It sells a number of volunteer vacations, in partnership with Conservation Volunteers International Program.

Jason's choice will depend on available funds, what his friends want to do, and how green he wants to be. But he sees he has a wide range of options, all of which could be designed with environmental protection in mind.

## CASE 5: GRACE MAKES A CASE FOR GREEN LIVING

Grace is a 17-year-old high school senior. She believes in protecting the environment. Her best friend Joe is convinced that it doesn't matter and that human actions have no effect on the world around us. She often finds herself in arguments with him.

Joe:       Why does the environment matter?
Grace:     We humans depend on the environment for our survival. We have to breathe air. We have to drink fresh water. We depend on plants for food—plants to eat ourselves, and to feed animals if we eat meat or eggs. If the water or air is polluted, or plants can't grow, then we will get sick or die.
Joe:       That sounds excessive. I don't see anyone dying from air pollution.
Grace:     But they are dying! The World Health Organization and the International Energy Agency estimate that in the 2010s, between 6 and 7 million people were dying every year because of air pollution. People in Delhi, India, can't leave their houses some days; when they do go out, they have to wear masks. Humans shouldn't have to die just so businesses can make money.

You may not see people dying in the United States, but that has happened too—back in 1948, 20 people died from air pollution in Donora, Pennsylvania. The town's steel mill and zinc plant were pumping out toxic gases—carbon monoxide, sulfur dioxide, and metal dust. A cold layer of air settled over the town and trapped those gases over it, forming a thick smog that burned everyone's eyes, nose, and throat. The zinc plant refused to shut down operations. The smog lasted five days, half the town got sick, and 20 people died. The hospital and morgue were both overwhelmed. This incident led to the federal and state governments passing laws regulating air pollution, which is why we don't have such a big problem today.

There are so many stories like this. In the 1950s, the cats of Minamata, Japan, suddenly came down with "dancing cat disease," in which they lost control of their bodies, stumbled, convulsed, and fell into the sea to drown. In 1956, the townspeople also started losing control of their bodies. They had convulsions, went into comas, and died. After thousands of people became ill, a doctor determined that a chemical plant had been dumping methylmercury into the ocean, poisoning the fish that fed cats and humans.

Joe: Lots of scientists don't think climate change is really happening.

Grace: No. That's simply not true. Scientists who study the climate overwhelmingly agree that the climate is changing and that humans are the primary cause. The consensus is over 90 percent—and among actively publishing climatologists, it's at least 97.5 percent. (And the scientists who are not in that majority all believe humans have some role; none of them think humans have no influence at all.) Scientists may disagree on certain specifics, such as the most likely increase in global temperature in the future, but they are not debating the basic conclusion. In fact, the consensus is so strong now that many researchers no longer bother mentioning it; instead, they focus on details, such as how fast the process is going and what the likely results will be.

It's simple enough, when you understand a little of how the atmosphere works. Carbon dioxide and methane are greenhouse gases that trap heat near Earth's surface. Fossil fuels contain large amounts of carbon that has been hidden underground for millions of years. When we take those fuels out of the ground and burn them, the combustion of carbon compounds with oxygen creates carbon dioxide and other greenhouse gases that end up in the air. The more carbon dioxide in the air, the hotter the planet gets.

People who imagine scientists don't agree on this don't understand how science works. Scientists do not take things on faith; they have to prove everything. That means thousands of people with advanced degrees in climate science are all looking at different versions of the data and coming to the same conclusion. They are not doing this because they want to—in fact, it could be wonderful for a scientist's career to disprove a common hypothesis—but because this is how every single experiment and study comes out. The addition of millions of years' worth of carbon to the air in just two centuries is having exactly the effect that would be predicted in a laboratory. Computer models are all predicting the outcomes that are appearing on the ground.

For example, the West Antarctic Ice Sheet is melting. Scientists have generated computer models showing that it is beginning to collapse. Predictions from 2016 suggest that if temperatures continue to climb and the ice sheets break apart, sea levels could rise 6 feet by the end of the 21st century—and the pace would pick up after that. That's a worst-case scenario, but even the best case would have water rising, and that is going to make a real difference to people living near coasts.

Scientists around the world are very concerned that humans are not paying enough attention to their warnings. Numerous scientific associations and academies in the United States and abroad have signed joint statements supporting the consensus that humans are causing global climate change. The people who know the most about how these processes work are the ones most worried about it. I think that's good reason to worry myself.

Joe:      Well, environmentalists all believe in evolution. If you believe in that, then you know that plants and animals will adapt to a changing world.

Grace:   They can't adapt that fast. Adaptation happens over generations, which can take hundreds or thousands of years. The world has changed much too fast for plants and animals to keep up.

Today humans have occupied over 80 percent of the world's surface, and we're using pretty much all the land in temperate and tropical areas. Forests have been cut down and prairies plowed under to make agricultural fields and urban areas. Highways crisscross the land, making it impossible for animals to travel through their former territories. Rivers and lakes are so developed that the species that lived in them have no more habitat. There is simply no place for wild organisms to go.

Climate change is making this worse. Plants have it especially hard because they can't move. If the climate gets too hot or too dry for them, they just die. If the temperature warms the 2°C that has been predicted for the 21st century, that will make the globe hotter than it has been in 3 million years. There weren't even any humans 3 million years ago. If the temperature increases 4°C, which is also possible, that will bring the climate back to where it was 35 million years ago—a time when almost nothing alive today existed. That would melt all the ice caps in the Arctic and Antarctic, raising sea levels considerably. We would see massive extinctions of species, with nothing to replace them. It might be very ugly.

And—to say someone "believes in evolution" is silly. Evolution is a scientific theory, which means it is a fact. It's not a matter of faith. Evolution is simply the principle that the inherited characteristics of a population change over time through generations. Anyone who has parents can see this in action—you are a different genetic being than either of your parents. Selection pressures determine which individuals survive and reproduce. The theory of evolution has been tested repeatedly and found to accurately predict outcomes, so much so that it is the foundation of the entire field of biology.

Joe: Environmentalists care more about valueless owls and mussels than about humans who need good jobs.

Grace: Seriously? Pollution is killing people now and you can actually suggest that caring about the environment is bad for humans?

It would be more accurate to say that people who don't care about the environment don't care enough about humans.

Someone has to point out environmental damage when it occurs. Avoiding that damage will almost always inconvenience some human. Cutting down old-growth forests endangers species like the spotted owl. Preventing logging in the owl's habitat will inconvenience some humans. There's no way around that.

Using stories like this to claim that environmentalists don't care about humans is unjustified and unfair. Environmentalists—even if they don't like to call themselves that—are concerned about the environment because they are themselves humans. Humans must have clean air and water in order to survive. A damaged environment can't provide those things.

And humans are flexible. Loggers and miners are capable of doing other jobs. They can move, while an old-growth forest can't. One of the advantages of being aware of our own existence is that we can make conscious choices about how to act. We can weigh costs and benefits. That sometimes means that loggers will lose their jobs—or maybe that logging business owners won't make an extra few million dollars. That may be a fair price for an irreplaceable functioning ecosystem.

Joe: I don't see how anything I do makes any difference. Why should I bother?

Grace: It's depressing to think about the world's problems. The glaciers are melting. Africa's 2017 population of 1.2 billion people may reach 2.4 billion by 2050, and maybe 4 billion by 2100. China is buying up African land and converting it to farmland for its own purposes—so how will those Africans feed themselves? The world's forests are being cut down to make things like disposable wooden chopsticks. A single oil spill can devastate hundreds of square miles of ocean. A tractor-trailer speeding down the highway at 75 mph produces far more emissions than a single family car driving cross-country for a vacation.

Composting the peel of one avocado and a tomato stem is not going to make up for the food wasted by all the fast-food restaurants in the city. When pollution streams out of industry and commerce all around the world far faster than individuals can recycle, the effort to live green can seem like a wasted sacrifice.

Is there any point in trying? Maybe we are doomed to watch as humans tip the balance of the next extinction and start dying in droves from the effects of climate change—which will include wars, mass migration, famine, starvation, epidemic diseases with no medical treatment. But some of us would prefer not to sit idly while that happens. We can see the causes in action, and we can study the science. We know that there are things that can be done to avert disaster. Real success will come only from a collective effort by people around the world. Those of us who live green now want to be part of that effort so that we can help, and we can influence others to join us.

### Analysis

Ignorance about the environment is widespread, and certain media outlets have made it their business to make sure that their viewers do not get accurate information. Facts are the best basis for arguing any point. Grace knows a great deal about her topic, and she is doing a good job of finding evidence to support her contentions.

Some would say that the best way to persuade others is to listen patiently to their point of view and try to make gentle and respectful arguments. Grace does a nice job of this. It is nice that she can be friends with someone who disagrees with her about certain facts that are thoroughly proven. Unfortunately, some people refuse to believe in facts or to trust scientists. That is a problem, because they influence policy by their votes. It is very frustrating to try to persuade people who do not want to be persuaded. You can't reason someone out of a position they didn't reason themselves into. Grace will do best to keep studying the science and following the issues and not backing down.

# Glossary

**Acid rain:** A form of precipitation that is significantly more acidic than neutral water, often produced as the result of industrial processes.

**Adaptation:** An inherited feature that helps an organism survive and reproduce in a particular environment or habitat.

**Air quality index:** Measurement of air quality, based on concentrations of surface ozone averaged over an eight-hour period for specific locations.

**Algae:** Plantlike organisms that live in water and perform photosynthesis.

**Anthropogenic:** Caused by humans.

**Aquatic:** In water; living in water.

**Aquifer:** An underground layer of spongy rock, gravel, or sand in which water collects.

**Atmosphere:** The layer of gases surrounding Earth; the air.

**Atom:** The smallest particle of a substance (i.e., an element), which cannot be broken by chemical means; composed of protons, neutrons, and electrons.

**Biofuel:** A fuel created from organisms that were alive fairly recently, such as wood, biodiesel, or bioethanol.

**Biomass:** Biological material derived from organisms that are still alive or were recently living, especially plants.

**Bycatch:** Animals that are caught in addition to the targeted fish species.

**Carbon:** Chemical element 6, an atom with six protons, the main component of living organisms and of fossil fuels.

**Carbon dioxide:** A molecule consisting of one carbon atom bound to two oxygen atoms; a significant greenhouse gas.

**Carbon footprint:** The amount of carbon dioxide and other carbon emissions produced by an activity or individual.

**Carbon monoxide:** A molecule consisting of one carbon atom bound to one oxygen atom.

**Carbon neutral:** Producing no net carbon emissions, whether by reducing emissions or by offsetting them in some way.

**Carbon offset:** A carbon sink, such as a forest, created to absorb the carbon emissions produced by a specific activity.

**Carbon sink:** Something that takes in and sequesters carbon from the air, such as a plant performing photosynthesis.

**Carbon source:** Something that emits gaseous carbon into the air, such as a machine that uses the combustion reaction of burning fossil fuels to produce energy.

**Chlorofluorocarbons (CFCs):** A group of organic compounds once used widely as propellants in commercial aerosol sprays but regulated in the United States since 1987 because of their harmful environmental effects.

**Clean Air Act:** Set of environmental regulations limiting pollutants emitted by cars, factories, and other sources. First enacted by the U.S. Congress in 1970 and updated several times since then.

**Climate:** The complete set of weather conditions in a region, including temperature, precipitation (rain or snow), air pressure, sunshine and cloud cover, and wind over a period of years.

**Climate change:** Significant change in climate patterns over time.

**Combustion:** Burning; a rapid chemical reaction called oxidation that produces heat and light.

**Crankshaft:** The component of an internal combustion engine that converts the up-and-down movement of the pistons into rotation.

**Cultivation:** Human-directed growth of domestic plants intended for human use.

**Data:** A set of pieces of information about a system, such as values at various times.

**Deforestation:** Total clearing of trees and other plants from forest areas.

**Desertification:** Transformation of arid or semiarid productive land into desert.

**Ecosystem:** All of the living and nonliving components of a particular area, including organisms, sun, air, soil, and water.

**Electric current:** A flow of electrons.

**Element:** A pure substance that cannot be changed chemically into a simpler substance; atoms are the smallest particles of elements.

**Emissions:** Substances discharged into the air as a byproduct of burning, such as the exhaust from a car engine, which contains carbon dioxide, carbon monoxide, and particulate matter.

**Energy:** Power that can be used to perform work.

**Environmental Protection Agency (EPA):** Government agency charged with implementing the provisions of the Clean Air Act.

**Erosion:** The wearing away of a surface by the action of wind, water, or ice.

**Ethanol:** An alcohol used as a fuel or fuel additive; also the main alcohol in alcoholic drinks.

**Evaporation:** The process by which a liquid changes into a gas.

**Extinction:** The end of a species, determined by the moment when the last member dies.

**Fertilizer:** A substance added to soil to encourage plant growth and to increase crop yields.

**Fossil fuel:** Fuels formed by the decomposition of dead organisms over several million years, including coal, petroleum, and natural gas.

**Glacier:** A river of ice that moves down a valley to the ocean, where it breaks off or "calves" into icebergs.

**Green:** Environmentally conscious; nonpolluting.

**Greenhouse gas:** A gas that traps heat in the atmosphere; the main greenhouse gases are water vapor, carbon dioxide, methane, and ozone.

**Habitat:** The natural environment in which a particular kind of organism lives.

**Hydrocarbon:** A molecule composed of hydrogen and carbon atoms.

**Ice Age:** A period of low temperatures that lasts for millions of years, resulting in the formation of polar ice sheets and glaciers.

**Ice cap/ice sheet:** A mass of ice that covers a large area of a landmass.

**Incineration:** Burning.

**Industrial Revolution:** The period from about 1760 to 1840 in which human societies rapidly started using machines for transportation and manufacturing.

**Internal combustion engine:** An engine in which the chemical reaction that supplies energy to the engine takes place within the engine itself.

**Landfill:** A waste disposal facility in which waste is densely packed and buried.

**Leaching:** The movement through soil of chemicals dissolved in water.

**Methane:** A chemical compound made of one carbon and four hydrogen atoms; a strong greenhouse gas.

**Migration:** The seasonal movement of a species from one habitat to another.

**Molecule:** A particle made by the chemical bonding of two or more atoms; the smallest particle of which a compound is made.

**Nuclear fission:** The splitting of an atomic nucleus, releasing large amounts of energy.

**Nuclear fuel:** A material that will engage in a fission reaction, mainly isotopes of the radioactive elements uranium and plutonium.

**Nuclear reactor:** A device that contains a nuclear reaction in order to harness the energy released by that reaction.

**Nucleus:** The cluster of protons and neutrons at the center of an atom.

**Old-growth forest:** A mature forest that has not been disturbed in a very long time, containing highly diverse tree species of all ages, multilayered canopies with many gaps, and high animal biodiversity.

**Organic:** Containing the element carbon; coming from an organism that is or was alive.

**Organic farming:** Farming that uses natural methods and substances to control pests and improve productivity and avoids the use of synthetic fertilizers and pesticides.

**Ozone:** A form of oxygen that consists of three atoms of oxygen per molecule, with the chemical formula $O_3$.

**Ozone layer:** A region of the upper atmosphere in which the concentration of ozone is significantly higher than in other parts of the atmosphere.

**Pesticide:** A substance used to eliminate pests such as insects, fungi, or weeds.

**Photosynthesis:** The process by which plants and algae use the sun's energy to convert carbon dioxide and water into sugars.

**Photovoltaic cell:** A solar cell; a light-sensitive device containing semi-conductor crystals (materials that conduct an electric current under certain conditions) that convert sunlight to electricity.

**Piston:** A solid object that fits inside a cylinder and moves up and down to turn the crankshaft.

**Polar region:** The region north of the Arctic Circle and south of the Antarctic Circle, with low temperatures year-round.

**Precipitation:** Condensed or frozen atmospheric water vapor that falls to the ground as rain, snow, sleet, or hail.

**Recycling:** Using waste material for another purpose.

**Reef:** A hard raised area beneath the ocean's surface, consisting of coral, rock, or other object.

**Sea level:** The average level of an ocean.

**Scientific theory:** A thoroughly proven explanation for some natural thing or occurrence, something that has been proven by experimentation and evidence so many times that there is virtually no possibility of its being disproven.

**Skin cancer:** A skin disease caused primarily by DNA damage resulting from exposure to the ultraviolet radiation in sunlight.

**Smog:** Hazy pollution caused by a combination of air pollutants and water vapor reacting with one another in urban areas.

**Soil:** The mixture of minerals and organic matter that form dirt, in which plants grow.

**Solar panel:** A device used to convert the sun's energy into electrical power; a photovoltaic panel.

**Solar power:** Power produced by collecting and harnessing the sun's energy.

**Stratosphere:** The part of the upper atmosphere between 9 and 18 miles above Earth's surface.

**Sustainability:** The use of resources and development of practices in a way that meets the needs of people alive today without making it impossible for future generations to meet those same needs.

**Topsoil:** The top layer of soil, containing the most organic matter and nutrients that plants need.

**Toxin:** A poisonous substance produced by a biological organism.

**Turbine:** An engine that turns in a circular motion when force is applied to it.

**Ultraviolet radiation:** Invisible light that is of a shorter wavelength than visible blue light that causes sunburn and skin cancer.

**Volatile organic compound (VOC):** An organic liquid that easily transforms to a gas.

**Weather:** The set of conditions of temperature, humidity, cloud cover, and wind speed at a given time and place.

**Windmill:** A machine with several sails affixed to a center point that uses wind to turn a machine such as a mill or a pump. Windmills used today to convert wind power into electricity are called wind turbines.

# Directory of Resources

**BOOKS AND ARTICLES**

Berry, Wendell (1977). *The Unsettling of America*. San Francisco, CA: Sierra Club Books.

Chrisafis, Angelique, and Adam Vaughan. "France to ban sales of petrol and diesel cars by 2040." *The Guardian*, July 6, 2017.

Colbert, Elizabeth (2006). *Field Notes from a Catastrophe*. London: Bloomsbury.

Colbert, Elizabeth (2014). *The Sixth Extinction: An Unnatural History*. New York: Henry Holt and Co.

Diamond, Jared (2011). *Collapse: How Societies Choose to Fail or Succeed*. New York: Penguin.

Kondo, Marie (2014). *The Life-Changing Magic of Tidying Up*. Berkeley, CA: Ten Speed Press.

Santer, Ben. "I'm a climate scientist. And I'm not letting trickle-down ignorance win." *Washington Post*, July 5, 2017.

Wilson, E. O. (2013). *The Social Conquest of Earth*. New York: Liveright.

Wilson, E. O. (2016). *Half-Earth: Our Planet's Fight for Life*. New York: Liveright.

**ORGANIZATIONS**

Environmental Protection Agency (EPA), www.epa.gov

The Environmental Protection Agency (EPA) is a federal government agency charged with enforcing regulations and laws that protect human health and the environment, including the Clean Air Act and the Clean Water Act.

Intergovernmental Panel on Climate Change (IPCC), www.ipcc.ch

The IPCC is a scientific body of the United Nations that provides objective analysis of climate change and environmental issues for member nations.

International Union for Conservation of Nature (IUCN), www.iucn.org

The IUCN is an international organization that gathers data and provides advocacy for the conservation of natural resources and living species.

Natural Resources Defense Council (NRDC), www.nrdc.org

The NRDC is a nonprofit international environmental organization that attempts to help governments and industry create sustainable environmental policies and practices.

The Nature Conservancy, http://www.nature.org/greenliving/

The Nature Conservancy is a charitable organization that focuses on land conservation.


## WEBSITES

Environmental Working Group (EWG), www.ewg.org

Food Waste Reduction Alliance, http://www.foodwastealliance.org/

Green Living Online, http://www.greenlivingonline.com

Green Restaurant Association, www.dinegreen.com

Green Seal, http://www.greenseal.org

The International Ecotourism Society (TIES), www.ecotourism.org

LEED, www.usgbc.org

Marine Stewardship Council, https://www.msc.org

National Center for Appropriate Technology, https://www.ncat.org

National Integrated Drought Information System (NIDIS), www.drought.gov

Passive House Institute, http://passivehouse.com

Projects Abroad, www.projects-abroad.org

Smarter Lunchrooms, https://www.smarterlunchrooms.org/scorecard-tools/smarter-lunchrooms-strategies

Terrapass, www.terrapass.com

U.S. Department of Agriculture, Organic Certification Made Simple, https://www.ams.usda.gov/reports/organic-certification-made-simple

U.S. Food Waste Challenge, https://www.usda.gov/oce/foodwaste

Whole Kids Foundation, www.wholekidsfoundation.org

# Index